action
for
wilderness

Seventh in the Sierra Club Battlebook Series

action
for
wilderness

edited by Elizabeth R. Gillette

Wilderness Conference, 12th
"' Washington, D.C., 1971,

Sierra Club   San Francisco • New York

The Sierra Club, founded in 1892 by John Muir, has devoted itself to the study and protection of the nation's scenic and ecological resources — mountains, wetlands, woodlands, wild shores and rivers. All club publications are part of the nonprofit effort the club carries on as a public trust. There are more than 40 chapters coast to coast, in Canada, Hawaii and Alaska. Participation is invited in the club's program to enjoy and preserve wilderness everywhere. Address: 1050 Mills Tower, San Francisco, California 94104; 373 Fifth Avenue, New York, N.Y. 10016, or 324 C Street, S.E., Washington, D.C. 20003.

This battlebook is printed on Valentine Precycle Offset. The paper is manufactured from a nonwood fiber called bagasse. Bagasse is the residue that remains after sucrose has been extracted from sugar cane. The environmental benefits of using Precycle Offset are multiple: bagasse traditionally is burned (causing air pollution) or used for landfill in the wetlands of the Southeast.

Copyright © 1972 by the Sierra Club.
All rights reserved.
Library of Congress catalog card number 79-189967.
International Standard Book number 87156-062-3.

Designed and produced by Charles Curtis, Inc., New York. Typeset in 11 point Press Roman on 13 points by Harold Black Inc., New York, and printed in the United States of America by Associated Book Company, Inc.

Contents

Foreword

Never before have public outcries against the would-be despoilers of wilderness been louder or more fierce than they are today. Quite probably never in our country's history have so many people recognized the need to set aside wilderness in perpetuity—to remove it from the marketplace, and to protect it once and for all from the ravages of timbering, mining and recreational development.

Yet, despite the inarguable need for wilderness and outspoken demands for its preservation, not enough progress is being made to preserve this resource for all time.

In 1964 Congress recognized that some additional, special, designation was urgently needed to help protect America's last wilderness. It established the National Wilderness Preservation System so that the wildest land within the national parks, forests, wildlife refuges and ranges could be preserved forever. Since 1964, however, both the U.S. Congress and the executive branch, by moving at a snail's pace, have kept the Wilderness Act from accomplishing what it was intended to do. Congress alone makes the final decision on whether to include an area in the Wilderness System; its activities in this field have been virtually at a standstill since 1970. Also under the provisions of the Wilderness Act certain federal agencies must review eligible land for possible inclusion in the system; this review process is far behind schedule. Unfortunately, the 1974 deadline for addition of appropriate areas to the Wilderness System is fast approaching.

This is a book on wilderness, but not one of the usual breed. It contains no dramatic wilderness photographs; it is a book for those people who already "believe." It is based on the premise that the survival of wilderness is too important to be left to the whims of congressmen and government agencies. The book is intended as a practical manual for activists, and activists-to-be, in their wilderness preservation campaigns.

What does action for wilderness entail? First, a knowledge of the laws—federal, state and local—affecting the area in question, because only through government regulation can wilderness be preserved in perpetuity. The environment activist will find in this book analyses of two major laws designed to protect wilderness in federal ownership—the Wilderness Act, and the National Wild and Scenic Rivers Act of 1968. Because wilderness legislation at the state level is extremely inconsistent in quality (or worse, nonexistent), it would be impossible to examine the laws in all fifty states. But one model piece of legislation is presented: a bill providing for the creation of a wilderness system in Michigan. This bill, introduced in the 1971 state legislature, concerns suitable land located within the boundaries of state parks and wildlife refuges. The book also explores a number of *ideas* for preserving wilderness acreage in private ownership. Such areas, though usually small, are nevertheless important as a wilderness resource.

So much for the laws. How well are they working? The activist must find out. (If there are no laws pertaining to his area of interest, his course of action will be obvious—lobbying for such legislation.) Do problems arise in the laws' implementation? What can the activist do to help solve them? The citizen must decide on the most effective role he can play in the effort, and then pursue it as expertly as possible. At the earliest stage of a preservation campaign the drawing up of a formal proposal to set aside a wilderness region under state or federal law provides an outstanding opportunity for citizen involvement: to make thorough field studies, which are the foundation of every wilderness proposal. At any rate, the activist should familiarize himself with all aspects of the land he intends to protect, for this expertise will serve as his entrée to government agencies and legislators. Chapter 5 is a step-by-step guide for such preparation and field work.

The next stage in the action campaign is to begin organizing broad support. Whose decisions will be important? Who in the community is in a position to influence those decisions? It is important to master the techniques of testimony described in Chapter 6 because public hearings as reported by television and newspaper media can play a crucial role in government decisions. And it is essential, both before and after hearings, to keep in close touch with the government officials who draft the final wilderness proposals.

Additional steps deserve to be taken. To avoid duplication of effort, every activists' group should find out whether other groups are working toward the same goal. When campaigns depend on volunteer services and sparse funds, coalitions of environmental groups are more effective than any single group can be. The national headquarters of the Sierra Club can supply names and addresses of other people who might already be working on the same cause.

All this involves a good deal of work. But citizens' campaigns across the nation have demonstrated that concerted action can direct, and successfully redirect, the final disposition of U.S. wilderness areas.

The above series of steps for wilderness action evolved from the Sierra Club's Twelfth Biennial Wilderness Conference held in Washington, D.C., on September 24 through 26, 1971. This book is based on the proceedings of that conference. But it represents a break with tradition. Unlike other wilderness conference books published during the previous twenty years, it does not contain the full conference proceedings. To produce a tight, succinct guide for waging wilderness campaigns, and in keeping with the Battlebook format, we have omitted some conference speeches and included certain supplementary articles. The conference participants whose material is not included here nevertheless made a distinct contribution with their many valuable comments, criticisms and suggestions.

Anyone who loves wilderness should plan to attend a Sierra Club wilderness conference. The conferences are the most effective forum today for the exploration of wilderness issues and problems by people from all fields—the political arena, business world, environmental organizations, and the very mountains, valleys, and deserts of the wilderness itself. The next Sierra Club wilderness conference will be held in Denver in 1974. Future conferences probably will be conducted in places other than California, Washington, or Denver, in order to provide more people with the opportunity of learning about wilderness. And the programs probably will emphasize local wilderness battles, as well as national ones.

Like so many endeavors in the name of conservation, wilderness conferences depend almost entirely on volunteers. Therefore a word of gratitude is in order to the helpful and enthusiastic group of volunteers in Washington, D.C., who worked on the 1971 conference. And to Conference Chairman James Gilligan. And to Lanphere Graff and Richard O'Brien, who helped greatly with the preparation of this book.

—Elizabeth R. Gillette

I.
The Wilderness Act:
An Analysis
and Assessment

What
the Wilderness Act
Means

By Michael McCloskey

The Wilderness Act, passed by Congress in 1964 as a
result of an eight-year campaign, was designed to provide a clear national policy that wilderness is a public
value deserving protection for all time under a systematic statutory program, the National Wilderness Preservation System.

Units initially included in the Wilderness System
when the act became law were 9.1 million acres in fifty-
four units of national forest lands then called wilderness
and wild areas. Also included at that time was the
Boundary Waters Canoe Area in Minnesota, subject to
fewer restrictions and increased in size administratively
in 1965. Not included in the Wilderness System but
accorded limited protection were 5.5 million acres in
thirty-four national forest areas then designated as primitive areas. This acreage is protected by law against log-

Mr. McCloskey is executive director of the Sierra Club. A complete text of
the Wilderness Act may be found as Appendix A, page 185.

ging, roads, motor vehicles and equipment but is still open to mining, licensed dams and utility installations.

Enlarging the Wilderness System has been and will continue to be a major effort for conservation groups around the country. In order to work effectively under the terms of the Wilderness Act, it is necessary to understand: the review processes (and to be involved in them when conditions warrant it); the necessary qualifications for placement of units in the Wilderness System; and the administrative requirements for managing the system.

Mandatory Reviews

All national forest primitive areas, all roadless units more than 5,000 acres in size within the National Park System and the National Wildlife Refuge and Range System (as these systems were constituted in 1964), and all roadless islands in the Refuge System are to be reviewed by the secretaries of agriculture and the interior respectively by 1974 to determine which units shall be recommended to Congress for inclusion in the Wilderness System. Each departmental secretary was to review one-third of the units affected by 1967, two-thirds by 1971 and the remainder by 1974 (by September 4 of each year).

The order of steps in the mandatory review process is as follows: (1) The administering agency (either the Forest Service, the National Park Service or the Bureau of Sport Fisheries and Wildlife) studies the unit and develops a proposal for inclusion in the Wilderness System. (2) The bureau chief approves the proposal. (3) The proposal is announced in the Federal Register, local newspapers and in an agency brochure. (4) State governors, the county governing board and other interested federal agencies are notified of the proposal and invited to comment on it. (5) Local administrative hearings are held, where a verbatim transcript of testimony is taken and letters are accepted for the hearing record. (6) The agency analyzes the hearing record, reassesses its proposal in the light of comments received and forwards a report and final proposal to the secretary of the department.

(7) The secretary reviews the agency recommendation and forwards it to the president. (8) The president reviews each secretarial recommendation and then forwards it to Congress, along with the hearing record. The president can administratively increase the size of primitive areas by up to 5,000 acres (providing no single unit is more than 1,280 acres) at the time he submits his proposal to Congress.

(9) Each presidential recommendation is usually introduced in Congress as a bill and referred to the Committees on Interior and Insular Affairs. (10) Congressional action in Washington, D.C., includes: hearings by both houses, as well as field hearings; committee mark-up sessions, with possible amendments; a report to the floor; floor debate, with possible amendments; passage by each house; and possible conference committee sessions to resolve differences. If a bill faces stubborn opposition within Congress, particularly within committees, it may never be reported out, or it may be emasculated by amendments. A bill also may not move because of insufficient public interest and support. (11) The president either signs or vetoes the bills passed by Congress.

Discretionary Reviews

While the Wilderness Act does not state clearly

whether additional units may be added to the system beyond those subject to mandatory review, there would seem to be no legal barrier to such additions. Conservationists are urging the Forest Service to propose a number of de facto wilderness units (areas in national forests that are of wilderness quality but lack any legal protection or designation to protect that quality) for inclusion in the Wilderness System. No clear policy exists with respect to wilderness zoning within national parks and wildlife refuges established after September, 1964. While there is no general requirement that the secretary of the interior forward wilderness recommendations on these, conservationists feel he should recommend wilderness zoning at the time these units are proposed, or within a short time after their establishment. In some instances Congress has asked for wilderness recommendations within two years following their establishment.

Qualifications for New Units

Agencies must look to the definition of wilderness set down in the Wilderness Act to assess whether primitive areas and roadless areas qualify for designation as wilderness areas. They must consider the following characteristics:

Land ownership. The potential wilderness area must be federally owned, though non-federally owned inholdings may exist within a minor share of the area. Although the act mentions only the holdings of the Park Service, Forest Service, and Bureau of Sport Fisheries and Wildlife, there would seem to be nothing to preclude Congress from adding holdings of other federal agencies, such as the Bureau of Land Management. Congressional action is mandatory if the holdings of other agencies are to be designated wilderness areas.

Condition. The land must appear to have been primarily affected by forces of nature, with man's impact substantially unnoticeable throughout the entire unit. There may be no permanent improvements, including permanent roads. There may be no human habitation on the federally owned land within the unit. And the unit should successfully maintain the natural community of life.

Potential use. The unit must have outstanding opportunities for solitude or a primitive and unconfined kind of recreation.

Size. The unit must be at least 5,000 acres in size or, if smaller, it must be large enough to be used but still feasibly preserved in an unimpaired condition.

Optional features. These include features of interest for scientific (including ecological and geological features), educational, conservation, scenic or historical reasons.

Administrative Requirements

While the administering agencies are charged with preserving the wilderness character of units in the system, nothing in the Wilderness Act overrides the general purposes for which national forests, national parks or wildlife refuges and ranges are established. Further, the act does not modify the special body of legislation governing the Boundary Waters Canoe Area (which allows logging and motor vehicles in specified sectors).

Under no circumstances are permanent roads allowed in wilderness areas. With exceptions that will be discussed later, the only commercial enterprises allowed are those servicing wilderness recreational users, such as packers, outfitters and guides. Commercial timber cutting, for example, is prohibited unless authorized by the secretary of agriculture in connection with a program to control fire, insects or disease. Presumably, noncommercial timber cutting is restricted only to the extent that it is inconsistent with preserving the wilderness in an unimpaired condition (for instance, cutting for firewood or construction timbers for agency use or cutting for research work might be permissible within this limitation). The following uses and facilities are *not* allowed for general public use, but can only be undertaken by the agency as required for administering the area (including use in emergencies): temporary roads, structures, installations, motor vehicles, motorized equipment, motorboats, aircraft landing and other forms of mechanical transport.

The administering agency, nevertheless, can use motorized equipment and build structures and temporary roads if these are unavoidably necessary to preserve the wilderness and protect the health and safety of visitors. In no event, though, can it build permanent roads. The secretary of agriculture is empowered to use any measures that may be necessary to control fire, insects and disease. No such provision is made for the interior secretary, although his other general statutory authorities may provide similar power. The secretary of agriculture is also empowered to allow, if he chooses, the continued use of aircraft and motorboats within the units Congress placed in the Wilderness System on September 4, 1964, where this use was already established.

Prospecting for mineral resources in a manner that is compatible with wilderness preservation (as through observation and sampling outcrops) can be continued indefinitely within national forest wilderness units.

Further, the U.S. Geological Survey and the Bureau of Mines are to plan and conduct recurrent surveys of the mineral values within national forest wilderness units. Until 1984, national forest wilderness units will be open to the filing of mining claims. For claims filed between 1964 and 1984 only the mineral rights can be patented. While machinery and motors can be used to develop claims, methods of access are subject to reasonable regulation. Moreover, the secretary can require that areas on claims disturbed by mining be restored as near as practicable to a natural condition. No new claims can be filed after the beginning of 1984.

Water projects such as dams and appurtenant utilities may be installed in national forest wilderness units upon a presidential finding that they are in the public interest. It is not clear whether a license from the Federal Power Commission must be obtained for such projects, or whether power or irrigation withdrawals in wilderness areas have been vacated.

Within national forest wilderness units, grazing is permitted to continue under reasonable regulations (these regulations allow only those facilities which already exist plus new ones needed to protect the wilderness, e.g., a drift fence in some cases).

Finally, private or nonfederal inholdings and facilities do not disqualify an area from the Wilderness System if their unnatural character is not substantially noticeable in the whole unit; e.g., a privately owned telephone line or water line does not disqualify an area. Prohibitions of uses and facilities within wilderness areas apply just to federal land; they do not apply to privately owned holdings or facilities. Customary means of access that are consistent with wilderness (such as horse and wagon) must be granted across intervening federal land for mining claims and occupied inholdings. For other unoccupied holdings only adequate access (such as by foot) must be afforded or land must be offered in exchange. As funds are appropriated by Congress, inholdings may be purchased by the federal government from willing sellers. Special congressional authorization is necessary for condemnation.

Is the Wilderness Act Working?

By Michael McCloskey

A little more than seven years ago, in Washington, D.C., the Wilderness Act was signed. Conservationists had hoped it marked the end of a long struggle—that with its passage the protection of wilderness would be assured. Instead, the Wilderness Act signaled the beginning of a new struggle.

This was so because conservationists were forced to accept a compromise in securing the act's passage. The compromise, demanded by the House Interior Committee Chairman, Wayne Aspinall, required congressional approval of every wilderness area added to the National Wilderness Preservation System. The requirement of "affirmative action by Congress in the designation of Wilderness Areas" was one of the political prices we had to pay to get the act through Congress.

It is time to recognize how high a price we paid. The

Mr. McCloskey presented this paper at the Twelfth Biennial Sierra Club Wilderness Conference, in Washington, D.C., on September 24, 1971.

burdens of seeking affirmative congressional action that have fallen upon the conservation movement have been heavy, and we all wondered at the outset whether we could carry them. But we have, and in the process our organizations—the Sierra Club, The Wilderness Society and others—have all grown stronger. In one sense the burdens have been good for us. They have deepened and strengthened the public's understanding of the need for wilderness. But the burdens have been growing, too. It is becoming increasingly difficult to overcome the obstacles in the way of timely and forthright congressional action.

By 1971, the seventh year out of ten provided for reviewing potential candidates for inclusion in the Wilderness System, federal agency reviews were to be two-thirds complete. Out of a total 179 areas, reviews on 119 should now be complete. To date, proposals have been forwarded to Congress on only 60. Congress in turn has acted on only 33. Out of the potential 66,440,387 acres, only 10,411,000 acres are now in the Wilderness System. The Forest Service has made the most progress: seven of its thirty-four primitive areas have been reclassified and added to the system, amounting to about one million acres. The Bureau of Sport Fisheries and Wildlife now has twenty-four units in the system, comprising only about 83,000 acres. The bulk of its acreage must still be processed. The National Park Service has had only two of its units added, totaling about 150,000 acres. More than 27 million acres of parkland remain to be processed; 21 million acres of refuges and some 7 million acres of Forest Service lands.

It is time to recognize that the formula for affirmative action is not working. It is apparent that the deadlines of the Wilderness Act will not be met. Probably all of the agency recommendations will not be before Congress by 1974.

In his Seventh Annual Report to Congress on the Status of the National Wilderness Preservation System, President Richard Nixon does not explain how the executive branch intends to meet the statutory schedule.[1] Only the Forest Service expresses the hope that it can meet the deadline. The National Park Service and the Bureau of Sport Fisheries and Wildlife make no effort to explain their situations. In fact, the Park Service is armed with a solicitor's opinion asserting that failure to meet the deadline does not really make much difference.

It is also apparent that neither the executive branch nor the Congress is trying to make the Wilderness Act work. Some persons in both branches may be trying, but the branches as a whole are not. Conservationists have been critical of the agencies and the National Park Service in particular in this regard. But it may be time to lay the blame where it most belongs—on Congress. Agencies are probably tailoring and limiting their proposals to suit powerful members of Congress because they know these members are not pressing for a larger Wilderness System.

Remember, Congress insisted on this agonizing review procedure. In its inherent design, the procedure is delay-oriented. By requiring every addition to the Wilderness System to run the twenty-four steps of the legislative

---

[1] The Wilderness Act requires that a jointly submitted annual report from the secretaries of agriculture and the interior on the status of the Wilderness System be transmitted to Congress by the president each year. Copies of the report may be obtained by writing the Secretary of Agriculture, Department of Agriculture, Washington, D.C. 20250; or the Secretary of the Interior, Department of the Interior, Washington, D.C. 20240.

gauntlet and countless other steps in the process of administrative review, Congress has maximized the opportunities for obstruction by our opponents. In each instance, there are more than two dozen chances for them to bottle up a proposal, and this bottling system is working with dismaying efficiency.

When the act was passed, conservationists feared this result. But we wanted to believe in the good faith of those who insisted that such a system of affirmative designation would work. Perhaps we had no alternatives then. But it is time to face reality. Representative Wayne Aspinall did not promise to enact most bills for additions to the Wilderness System. He said only that "none of these added areas can be classified as Wilderness or incorporated into the Wilderness System except by Act of Congress." He did not predict what Congress would do when it got the proposals. Now, we see that Congress has added thirty-three areas totaling 1.2 million acres to the Wilderness System—2 percent of the potential acreage that might be in the system. With 67 percent of the time elapsed, Congress has added only 2 percent.

Clearly, there is a demonstrable lack of leadership in Congress in processing wilderness legislation in a fashion that keeps faith with the intent of the Wilderness Act. Moods of congressional committees range from desultory to intractable. No action on wilderness legislation has been scheduled in the House of Representatives this session, with the exception of three items carried over from last year. Further progress may be held up for years over disputes on legislation stemming from the report of the Public Land Law Review Commission.[2]

[2] The Public Land Law Review Commission, headed by Congressman Wayne Aspinall, was established by Congress in 1964 to study most feder-

While the Senate has moved somewhat faster its record is still not good. Some bills have languished before the Senate Interior Committee through three Congresses. Continued progress is likely to be slow because many remaining wilderness area proposals are among the most controversial.

Rather than exhaust our energies in trying to hasten congressional action, it is time to correct the flaw in the Wilderness Act that required this agonizingly slow procedure in the first place.

We have embarked upon this effort. The Sierra Club was instrumental in putting a proposal before President Nixon for an executive order to preserve the status quo on all roadless portions of national parks and wildlife refuges and in roadless areas adjoining primitive areas until the president and Congress determine their suitability for inclusion in the Wilderness System.[3] In this way, wilderness would be preserved until a proposal is finally acted upon. The secretary of agriculture also would be directed to inventory and protect all other de facto wilderness in the national forests.

Although this executive order has not yet been signed, it has the backing of the Council on Environmental Quality and the secretary of the interior. It faces opposition from the secretary of agriculture, the Forest Service and the forest products industry. The order asks

ally owned lands in the United States and to recommend the best ways of utilizing them for maximum public benefit. The commission's final report, "One Third of the Nation's Land," which was released June 23, 1970, has generated heated controversy over its land use recommendations. Copies of the report are available at the Government Printing Office, Washington, D.C. 20402, at $4.50 each.

[3] For a complete text of the proposed Presidential Executive Order on Wilderness, see Appendix C, page 220.

no more than that our opportunities be respected while we deliberate. Nothing could be more basic to the deliberative process than to preserve the subject matter while a debate is underway.

If the president fails to act—and he has the authority to do so under the broad organic acts for the agencies involved—then our only option is to try to amend the Wilderness Act itself. Despite the act's original flaws we were reluctant to face this prospect until now. We felt it should be given a fair chance and that we should not risk exposing ourselves to the possibilities of further weakening amendments. But I believe we are now strong enough to block any setback, and this act has been tried and found wanting.

We need an omnibus amendment to the Wilderness Act placing all of our proposed units in the Wilderness System. The amendment should also require congressional action only to override agency action; it should extend interim protection to de facto wilderness until proposals are forthcoming and disposed of; it should end the special dispensations for mining in wilderness areas (mining is allowed in national forest wilderness areas until 1984) and provide a program to condemn the miners' inholdings; and it should clarify various technical questions relating to administration of the Wilderness System.

While the campaign for a new and better Wilderness Act will be long and arduous, the sooner we begin the better. This effort at reform should be the conservationists' answer to the failures of Congress and the executive branch to keep faith with the goals of 1974. We should look to 1974 as the beginning of a well-planned campaign for these reforms.

Our wilderness can only be as safe as our legal tools are fit to protect it. Clearly, these tools are not adequate now. Let us begin the quest for the tools we need. We will not have a generous legacy of wilderness unless we get them. Our need for wilderness demands that we do.

Preserving
Wilderness in the Northwest

By Brock Evans

I have never forgotten my first meeting nearly five years ago with the supervisor of the Willamette National Forest in Oregon. He put his feet up on his desk, leaned back and said, "I don't like you people. I'm not going to let you lock up any more wilderness." And he referred to the Oregon Cascades wilderness as a "forest slum."

I came out of that meeting full of fight, determined that he was not going to succeed. Also, I was relieved, having finally seen the face of the enemy we were up against. Nearly everywhere in the Northwest it seemed that the wilderness concept—at least where it involved extractable resources—was under full assault, and the picture was grim.

But something has happened in the years since then. Looking back now, a most remarkable change seems to have taken place in the Northwest.

Mr. Evans is the northwest representative of the Sierra Club. This paper was presented at the Twelfth Biennial Sierra Club Wilderness Conference, in Washington, D.C., on September 24, 1971.

We won in the North Cascades: we got our national park and wilderness areas. And now, strong local organizations are defending other areas in need of protection. The Oregon Cascades issue has been reopened, and thousands of people are involved in it now. We're going to save French Pete Creek valley somehow, and in Hells Canyon the dams will not be built. The situation in Idaho has changed so much that recently Senator Frank Church, at hearings to help determine the fate of Hells Canyon, spent a good deal of his time refuting the claims of witnesses testifying against putting the area into the Wilderness System. The Idaho senator said that in his state there is a gut feeling that all the rest of the wilderness should be saved, and that this was the result of no organized campaign, but rather a deep feeling for wilderness on the part of the people. This is in one of the most extraction-oriented of all western states.

How has it happened that there has been such a reversal of opinion? There are a host of reasons, some more complex than others. But throughout is one simple fact: the people—real people, not the chamber of commerce establishment but the men on the street—are with the conservationists. Conservationists in the Northwest were forced to go directly to the people, to meet with them to try to get them to express their feelings for wilderness. We had to offset the organized power of the special interest lobbies; and this has been done—all over the country, not just in the Northwest. By going straight to the people at county fairs and in movies, through the press and television, in countless meetings in small towns, a tremendous wellspring of latent feeling was opened up and is now with us.

Perhaps Representative Wayne Aspinall did conservationists more favors by the 1964 Wilderness Act than they realized. The rigid requirements that he as House Interior Committee Chairman implemented for hearings and reviews at all levels have made us lean and strong, and forced us to go to the grass roots, where we are now and are not to be dislodged. People want wilderness. It is expressed everywhere; it is expressed in every poll run by northwestern congressmen, even in the most timber-oriented districts.

We have broken the power of the antiwilderness lobbies—the timber and mining and grazing and dam-building people. Not completely, but we have broken it nevertheless. There is still sentiment against wilderness, to be true, but as I see it we clearly have the upper hand. Public support for wilderness is overwhelming: the people *are* with us.

Given these strong manifestations of public support to preserve more wilderness, we would expect the federal agencies that have wilderness to protect—the National Forest Service and the National Park Service, in particular—to be moving rapidly in the direction of following the public will, wouldn't we?

We would expect that the procedures outlined in the Wilderness Act that require review of primitive areas and portions of the national parks would be expedited. We would expect that the ensuing agency recommendations would include maximum amounts of wilderness for the National Wilderness Preservation System. Even more important, we would expect that de facto wilderness on Forest Service lands would be administered for protection until Congress has enough time to enact protective legislation. There are at least six to eight million acres of de facto wilderness at stake here—that is, land which is in fact wilderness, but because of its location is not subject to review under the 1964 Wilderness Act.

This is what we would expect. Unfortunately, it is not what is happening. The problem is not so much the procedures of the Forest Service or the Park Service. Both agencies apparently have well-developed techniques to inventory the wilderness resource. The Forest Service in particular has a high degree of competency in this regard and is on schedule with its required reviews. The Park Service has had difficulty meeting its schedule and its delays in some instances are inexcusable.

Instead, the problem is the agencies' attitude toward wilderness. In my opinion the Forest Service is more at fault in this respect than the Park Service. Park Service recommendations for the Wilderness System are not necessarily adequate and there are serious problems with its orientation. But there is more acreage at stake, and much more acreage recently threatened by the attitude of the Forest Service. Basically the attitude is characterized by a strong bias against formal wilderness area designation by statute if there are other resources, especially timber, that can be taken out of that area. This "timber first" attitude crops up in nearly all wilderness controversies involving the Forest Service despite recent national controversy over logging and clear-cutting in national forests. When the arguments against including a certain area in the Wilderness System are stripped away, it usually comes down to the fact that the area in question contains commercial timber which can be logged— and that is the real reason the Forest Service objects to wilderness classification.

The Forest Service is a forestry-logging agency still, dominated at all decision-making levels by foresters who contend, "Trees are a crop, and the big ones are going to go to waste unless they're harvested." Recently I heard this statement twice from the chief himself, as he testified on proposals to protect the Oregon Dunes and Hells Canyon.

There is additional evidence of this attitude. A few years ago I conducted a survey and found that nowhere in the Northwest has the Forest Service ever voluntarily set aside for the Wilderness System any substantial area of forest, if that forest could be logged at the time it was set aside, without enormous public pressure. Recent recommendations of the Forest Service for reclassification of primitive areas also point this out.

The Sawtooth area in central Idaho, for example, contains 200,000 acres of splendid country, mostly rocks. Two or three little valleys on the west side have some fine stands of ponderosa pine which are now within the present primitive area boundaries. But the Forest Service proposal for the Wilderness System omitted 13,000 acres of these ponderosa pine valleys, saying, "The area is not of wilderness quality." We know better.

The Mount Jefferson Wilderness Area of Oregon includes few big Douglas fir despite enormous public sentiment in favor of protecting these splendid forests. The boundaries set in 1968 followed Forest Service recommendations which excluded commercial timberlands. Now, the Forest Service is permitting logging in choice de facto wilderness next to the boundary, over conservationists' protests—places which should be in the Wilderness System.

The Forest Service's attitude toward de facto wilderness is even more important. It is most serious; final battles are being waged every day. There is no statutory obligation to study de facto wilderness. Until very recently, there were no procedures to study or even identify this resource. In fact, over the years most of the countryside was committed to logging and thereby placed in the allowable cut. Valley after valley of splendid wilderness has been logged despite our protests. It is still happening in Alabama as well as Oregon, Wyoming as well as West Virginia, and in California as well as Alaska.

There is a curious double standard here: on the one hand, if we conservationists want more wilderness preserved we have to go through endless reviews and hearings, exposed at every step of the way to full-scale attack by industry. On the other hand, if de facto wilderness is to be logged there are no hearings or reviews whatsoever, no chance for public scrutiny except in the most *pro forma* sense. So conservationists have been forced to develop their own procedure to protect de facto wilderness. Basically, it consists of two steps: (1) We do our own studies of areas and make formal proposals to the Forest Service for their management. I call this the "drawing the line in the dust with our toes" procedure. We say, "This is the line, and we'll fight beyond this." Often we do have to fight, as in the Mount Jefferson Wilderness Area, the North Cascades, the Saint Joe in Idaho, and many other places. (2) If we get no satisfaction from the Forest Service, we attempt to get legislation introduced in Congress. In the Northwest we have followed this pattern for the Lincoln Backcountry, the Cougar Lakes, the Oregon Cascades and others.

This is not a terribly satisfactory procedure, because we do not have the manpower or the money to study every area in depth. There are at least seventy-five de facto wilderness units in Montana alone, for example. And we have to battle the agency every step of the way—because in effect the decision to log, sooner or later, has already been made. We see the pattern in the Alpine Lakes region of Washington, for example, where last summer as soon as conservationists advanced a proposal and requested deferral of controversial timber sales, the supervisor of the Wenatchee National Forest immediately notified his constituent timber industry and local officials opposed to wilderness classification, and raised quite a storm.

It is happening now in the Mount St. Helens area of the Gifford Pinchot National Forest in Washington. The Forest Service intends to permit logging in an area conservationists have proposed as a national monument. It is happening every day, too, in de facto wilderness that we haven't had a chance to study in depth. It is particularly serious in southeast Alaska.

Conservationists don't like this procedure; we'd like to have the assurance that in every area statutory procedures permitting all of us our say would be required.

Recently, the Forest Service appears to be moving in this direction. In February, 1971, the chief issued a directive ordering the service to identify areas of de facto wilderness suitable for wilderness classification. This was a fine step, and the Sierra Club commended it at the time. But there is a problem. The Forest Service will not use the review criteria specified in the Wilderness Act, which simply calls for protection of areas that are roadless and where the works of man are substantially unnoticeable. Instead, the Forest Service has proposed its own criteria, including such aspects as "suitability," "need," and "conflicts with other resources."

In other words, we are probably not going to get

adequate review or withholding of activities such as logging on all de facto wilderness. We are going to get it only on areas the Forest Service considers "suitable." This relates directly to the critical question of attitude. It is like letting the fox guard the henhouse and allowing him to determine how many hens he will not eat. The Forest Service will make the political judgment about an area and then study it. We don't want this—its proposals for the Wilderness System in the past have been exclusively "wilderness on the rocks," with the timbered valleys left out. We predict it will be the same in the future. It is only when we bring great pressure to bear that the Forest Service considers that forests might also belong in the Wilderness System.

Closely tied to what I consider to be the most critical wilderness problem today, de facto wilderness on national forest lands, is the subject of administering areas within the Wilderness System. The administration or the caretaking of an area classified under the Wilderness Act is generally very good. The Forest Service does a particularly fine job of managing this resource, and the Park Service basically does, too.

But the question of attitude toward wilderness creeps in here as well. It affects deeply our efforts to protect more of the wilderness resource. The Forest Service has a "purist" approach to wilderness. In some respects it is far more purist than most of us want.

Even though the Wilderness Act permits existence of prior nonconforming uses, structures and facilities within a wilderness area if they are necessary to maintain and administer the wilderness resource, the Forest Service follows regulations that restrict almost any mark of man. Some might say this is good—and perhaps it is in the long run. But it is not good as long as six to eight million acres of de facto wilderness are sitting unprotected. It is not good when we have to convince people that putting an area into the Wilderness System is a good idea—that they can still enjoy the wilderness and won't be barred from entering or using it, only restricted from nonconforming activities that could be harmful to the resource.

In fact, the Forest Service has used the purist concept to argue against wilderness areas in southeast Alaska—pointing to existing cabins in extremely isolated areas erected for protection against brown bears and the damp climate. It also complains that wilderness designation will prohibit planes from flying into the area, thus making management difficult. Southeast Alaska does have a unique climate and access problem. But the Forest Service's attitude contrasts greatly with the Park Service's policy in southeast Alaska. The Park Service's proposal for wilderness classification in Glacier Bay National Monument permits patrol cabins, limited facilities for pack stock control, and trailside shelters where necessary.

A similar situation exists in the south forty-eight states, where horse use can have damaging impact on fragile high country. The Forest Service wants some control facilities such as hitching racks and corrals, but contends that they cannot be present in wilderness areas because of the way it interprets the Wilderness Act. In fact, the Wilderness Act does not bar such structures from wilderness areas. Thus the Forest Service argues against wilderness classification through a faulty interpretation of the 1964 act. The effect is to turn horsemen and guides against wilderness designation. In existing units such as the Eagle Cap Wilderness in Idaho, the Forest Service tells horsemen that the horse-care facilities are going to have to go.

This excessive purism has one basic thrust: to keep more areas out of the Wilderness System.

The urgency of the present situation lies not so much in present procedures, which are basically good. Nor is it in the administration of wilderness areas *per se*, because that also is basically good, although the excessive purist interpretation of the Wilderness Act will do long-range harm to the wilderness idea and the possibility of preserving much more. Rather, the problem is one of attitude, an attitude which views wilderness classification as a threat to management flexibility, as something unwanted, or as somehow removing areas from "management"—especially if the areas could otherwise be logged.

It is difficult to change attitudes but conservationists can work to change structures and personnel, or force a change in the regulations. I would like to offer a few modest proposals to accomplish these goals:

(1) A lawsuit. Conservation groups should seriously consider legal action to challenge the Forest Service's interpretation of the Wilderness Act. The act does not say the Forest Service must be so inflexible, so let's get a court interpretation to know where we stand under the act.

(2) Removing the political decision-making power from foresters. With all respect to my many friends who are foresters, there is no inherent reason why foresters should make decisions—even preliminary ones—which then have the weight of a powerful agency behind them. My experience has been that however objective foresters may think they are, they do look at wilderness quite

differently from the rest of us. Management of the wilderness resource is indeed a matter for professionals, and requires expertise which should be entrusted to the land managers. But the fundamental decisions that determine allocation of these areas, that determine which areas will be preserved and which will not, are not the proper province of any specialty, especially one where all the background training has been to treat trees as an extractive resource.

Conservationists should consider some mechanism whereby the inventories and analyses are made by the same people as at present, but the final decision to allocate and the final recommendations are made by those attuned to the need for wilderness protection—people like sociologists, philosophers and laymen. If we must, let's have a new agency, a new bureaucracy, that is dedicated to searching for new wilderness. The Forest Service has for so long acted as an agency on behalf of the timber industry that it is obviously difficult for it *not* to favor logging forests. Maybe conservationists need a Wilderness Agency to build a bureaucratic empire—for us, this time.

(3) A mechanism to halt attrition of de facto areas. The logging and road-building are going on in de facto wilderness every day; there are moratoriums on only a few areas right now. If we can't get a moratorium by legislation, perhaps we'll have to take legal action against the agencies, before they irrevocably commit these resources.

I think we have a legal right to a permanent, substantial resource of wilderness in this nation. It is part of our basic right as a people, because wilderness is a part of us deeply rooted in our own culture. It is as much a part of our history as palaces and museums are to other, older cultures.

In the last third of this century, we are going to see the final closing off of this frontier—the truly last frontier. I think we have only one decade, and then it will be safe, or gone forever. We must not let the wilderness places die; we must make certain that they live.

I am weary of last-ditch battles and lawsuits. I am tired of the endless arguing about how pure a wilderness *should* be, while those who argue for its purity permit it to be logged.

No apologies for loving the earth, or for loving our wilderness, are necessary. We are all going to have to fight much harder, and I think we will win eventually— because the people are with us.

Preserving Southeastern Wilderness

By Theodore A. Snyder, Jr.

A number of wilderness action programs are going on in the southeastern United States, but none has been concluded, successfully or otherwise. Why? The problems conservationists face and the results of our efforts to preserve wilderness are clearly illustrated by three on-going campaigns: (1) the proposed Joyce Kilmer Wilderness Area in the Nantahala National Forest, North Carolina, and the Cherokee National Forest, Tennessee; (2) the proposed Sipsey Wilderness Area in the Bankhead National Forest, Alabama; and (3) wilderness area proposals for parts of the Great Smoky Mountains National Park.

In all three, the Forest Service has impeded and attempted to block wilderness designation by means of a stretched, unrealistic interpretation of the Wilderness

Mr. Snyder is a regional vice-president of the Sierra Club and chairman of its Joseph Le Conte Chapter in North and South Carolina. This paper was presented at the Twelfth Biennial Sierra Club Wilderness Conference, in Washington, D.C., on September 25, 1971.

Act. Its attitude is shaped by the opinion that there is
no wilderness in the Southeast. The law is then extended to justify that baseless opinion.

Disagreement between conservationists and the Forest Service focuses on the definition of wilderness. The
Wilderness Act reads:

> A wilderness, in contrast to those areas where
> man and his own works dominate the landscape, is
> hereby recognized as an area where the earth and
> its community of life are untrammeled by man,
> where man is a visitor who does not remain. An
> area of wilderness is further defined to mean . . . an
> area of undeveloped federal land retaining its pri-
> meval character and influence, without permanent
> improvements or human habitation, which is pro-
> tected and managed so as to preserve its natural
> conditions and which (1) generally appears to have
> been affected primarily by the forces of nature,
> with the imprint of man's work substantially un-
> noticeable; (2) has outstanding opportunities for
> solitude or a primitive and unconfined type of rec-
> reation; (3) has at least five thousand acres of land
> or is of sufficient size to make practicable its pres-
> ervation and use in an unimpaired condition; and
> (4) may also contain ecological, geological or other
> features of scientific, educational, scenic, or histor-
> ical value.

What happens when local citizens and conservationists try to save what appears to the ordinary observ-
er to be wilderness? From the Forest Service we get one
of two answers: either "The works of man have marked

it," or "It is far too small, nothing near 5,000 acres."
Let's examine these assertions one at a time.

Wilderness, first of all, is an area that generally appears to have been affected primarily by the forces of nature, with the imprint of man's work substantially unnoticeable. The Forest Service seizes on the word "primeval" and closes its senses to anything but virgin forest. In the East, it is a fact that virtually all the forested lands have been timbered, in marked contrast to the western United States. Nearly all the eastern mountain forests were stripped of their virgin cover between 1890 and 1940. This logging was done mostly by "cut out and get out" operators who clear-cut the forest, using logging railroads to extract the trees. Miles of old railroad grade remain in what otherwise may appear to be mature forest.

What happens when we propose such an area for inclusion in the Wilderness System? Several years ago conservationists proposed the creation of a Joyce Kilmer Wilderness Area combining Joyce Kilmer Memorial Forest and the valley of Slickrock Creek which adjoins it. The valley of Slickrock Creek lies in western North Carolina with a portion in Tennessee where the creek marks the state line. This roadless valley of 10,700 acres is entirely Forest Service land. At the turn of the century a logging railroad was built in the valley and logging begun. Calderwood Dam was built a short time later, and in 1922 logging operations had to cease when the trestle over the Little Tennessee River was covered by rising lake water. The loggers left behind 3,000 acres of virgin timber in the upper reaches of the valley as well as their old railroad grade. They took out all their rails, locomotive and rolling stock.

This fertile valley receives up to eighty inches of rain each year. In the fifty years since logging ceased, the forest has regrown where it was cut. Groves of poplars, up to two feet in diameter, give a cathedral-like setting to the valley. The crossties have rotted and the old railroad grade has been converted into a smooth hiking trail. The cuts and fills are smoothed and grown over, too. No traces remain of any buildings the loggers may have used.

Yet, when conservationists proposed that the valley of Slickrock Creek be preserved as part of the Wilderness System, we were told that it did not qualify. The trees, except for 3,000 acres of them at the upper end, were not virgin timber, the Forest Service said. Trees only fifty years old were the mark of man's hand in cutting virgin timber. And so was the old railroad grade. Unerasable, it said, thereby disqualifying the area from the Wilderness System for all time.

Another example of determined refusal to construe the Wilderness Act realistically was brought to light in the case of the proposed Sipsey Wilderness Area in the Bankhead National Forest, Alabama.

When conservationists asked the Forest Service to set aside this 11,000-acre tract, we were told categorically that no forest land meeting the standards of the Wilderness Act could possibly exist in Alabama, although Forest Service personnel admitted they had not examined the area for potential wilderness designees. They pointed out that the land had been briefly farmed and a few wagon roads built. On this basis, they concluded that no land in Alabama could qualify for the Wilderness System.

The Forest Service obstinately refuses to look at any portion of the Sipsey that is not virgin in every respect.

Even then, it refuses to recognize that even 400 acres of virgin timber exist, when the total is actually closer to 5,000. It chooses to ignore the thirteen gorges that would be protected and their exceptional geological and botanical features. Instead, it concentrates on traces of old farms and logging roads, and the evidence of timber cutting visible only to an expert.

If areas once cut over are excluded from the operation of the Wilderness Act, then at a stroke nearly all wilderness in the Southeast is excluded. This narrow interpretation ignores the biological facts of life. Southeastern forests have fertile soil and a high rainfall which encourage rapid growth. In thirty to fifty years southeastern forests regrow and regenerate to the point where trees provide the full scenic beauties of wilderness. In that time new trees cover and heal the scars of earlier logging, effectively erasing the marks once laid on by the hand of man.

The classification of old, overgrown roads and railroad beds as disqualifying "works of man" is one example of this unrealistic interpretation. The railroad grades in the Slickrock drainage and the roads in Sipsey have been restored to nature. The banks are overgrown. The few cuts into rock have aged and are covered with moss, ferns and lichens. Even the Great Smoky Mountains National Park is laced with old railroad grades. And one of the two designated wilderness areas in North Carolina, Shining Rock, has an old railroad grade down its middle. These grades have been so restored to nature that they are no longer recognizable to the ordinary hiker. Additional wilderness designation is being refused, then, not because of works of man but rather by man's hypertechnical interpretation of the law.

Legislation has been introduced in Congress to include the Sipsey Wilderness Area in the National Wilderness Preservation System. Citizens were forced to go over the heads of public officials who should have been responsible. But conservationists are not always fortunate enough to be able to do so. In the case of the Joyce Kilmer Wilderness, the key support of the local congressman has been silently withheld. While other congressmen no doubt could be persuaded to introduce appropriate legislation, the endorsement of the local representative is critical and its absence nearly always fatal.

The second haggling response we get to requests for including southeastern areas in the Wilderness System is that the area is "too small" and therefore unqualified. Yet, the Wilderness Act defines wilderness as an area which has at least 5,000 acres *or is of sufficient size as to make practicable its preservation and use in an unimpaired condition*. In the Southeast the Forest Service has read as far as the words "5,000 acres" and put a period there. It obstinately refuses to consider any area less than that size.

The history of lumbering in the Southeast has already been mentioned. The areas that escaped the forages of the timber industry are but bits and scraps. They are corners that were overlooked, or were too remote or too difficult to log. For the most part they have been preserved by accident, not by design. Thus, a 5,000-acre area in its primeval state is exceptionally rare. However, a number of smaller areas are big enough to make their preservation in an unimpaired condition practicable and worthwhile.

Joyce Kilmer Memorial Forest in western North Carolina constitutes the entire watershed of Little Santeetlah

Creek. It is a whole geographic unit, extending from the ridge above its highest spring down to the creek's confluence with Santeetlah Creek. But the problem is this: the entire watershed, from side to side, top to bottom, covers only 3,800 acres.

The area is too small, we were told, to be made a unit of the Wilderness System. Manifestly, it is an ideal unit for consideration. Its area is ample; it is a natural geographic unit. The only thing that has prevented its protection within the Wilderness System has been an interpretation of the Wilderness Act made by public officials wearing blinders.

Another sop thrown out in response to our request for wilderness classification was that Kilmer would be equally well preserved by administrative protection. (Once land is made a unit of the National Wilderness Preservation System it is protected *by law* against encroachment by man.) Let's see how "administrative" protection compares with the legal kind. The Forest Service's printed brochure about Kilmer states, "No plant living or dead may be cut or removed." Guess who was the first to violate that principle? Government surveyors have been allowed to cut and remove all the living and dead plants they desire in making a survey across Kilmer—the prelude to construction of a commercial highway through the unprotected wilderness. This should not have happened, and would not have if the Wilderness Act had been fairly read and applied to areas of less than 5,000 acres.

Conservationists have proposed that this highway be restored to its originally planned route through another valley—not roadless—now devoted to timber production. We pointed out that the virgin forest of Kilmer adjoins the roadless valley of Slickrock Creek and that the 3,000 acres of virgin timber in.Slickrock are along the common boundary. Combining the two would rule out any objections as to size: there would then be *more* than 5,000 contiguous acres of virgin timber. The combined area of 14,500 acres is entirely roadless. As public protest became apparent, the government reduced its planned invasion of Joyce Kilmer from 200 acres to 60 to 40 to 15. But it has refused to remove the rerouted road from the high narrow ridge which forms the common boundary between these two wilderness units.

To prevent this destruction fourteen local and national conservation organizations joined together under the name "Joyce Kilmer Wilderness Advocates" to get these areas permanently protected as one unit in the Wilderness System. A brochure was printed and widely distributed. But letters and petitions from an estimated 10,000 persons have so far failed to sway government officials. We succeeded in getting the government to agree to prepare an Environmental Impact Statement on the road. It is still in preparation and I cannot hazard a guess as to what it will contain, but I know what it should contain. It should recognize that the proposed road will ruin forever two rare wilderness units, and recommend relocation of the road to land that has long since lost its wilderness character.

So far the problems cited have been limited to de facto wilderness. The Wilderness Act requires the Forest Service to study only those areas classified as "primitive" as of September 3, 1964. There were no primitive areas in North Carolina, South Carolina, Georgia or Alabama on that date. This was due in large measure to the practice of the Forest Service of making every decision in favor of large-scale timber production and none in favor of any other forest use value.

Despite enormous public demand to put Kilmer and Sipsey in the Wilderness System, nothing to this effect has been done by the Forest Service. Congressional legislation can be a material aid in these campaigns, as in the case of the Sipsey. But we need a remedy that does not require the favor of the local delegation in every instance. The need for wilderness is universal and its survival should not depend on the whim of one congressman or senator.

We need two things in order to protect potential wilderness areas on Forest Service lands in the Southeast. One is a fair interpretation of the definition of wilderness now written into the Wilderness Act. As long as the act is interpreted out of existence, the hopes for wilderness preservation are slim. The other great need is for an executive order on wilderness giving temporary protection to all areas of wilderness quality, regardless of size, and requiring a full-scale wilderness review of each of them.

My discussion would not be complete without some mention of the Great Smoky Mountains National Park. This is the most heavily used of all our national parks, yet not one acre of it is in the Wilderness System. A wilderness review study was made by the National Park Service in 1966. It proposed far too little acreage, so conservationists suggested an alternate plan. To this date, nothing has been done. The Park Service contends it is waiting until the controversy over the second transmountain road is settled. This, though, is a weak avoidance of the mandate of the Wilderness Act.

What has happened while the Park Service delays?

The service has graded out and widened miles of trail, making them into jeep roads. It has proposed monstrous developments inside park boundaries in areas of wilderness quality. It has proposed "motor nature trails" looping for miles through virgin forest. We must remember that the loggers were deep inside the Smokies before the park was created, and only about one-third of the area is virgin forest. The balance was logged, some even after creation of the park. The service has proposed a scenic highway circling the Smokies but would put part of it inside the park. One such place is along the Cataloochee Divide where the road would be visible from half the park and at the same time destroy a ridge-crest trail. Miles of "scenic" highway have been built but no funds spent on maintenance of hundreds of miles of trail. The result is that the roads are open, but the trails are closed. This reluctance of our public servants to comply with the letter or the spirit of the law cannot be explained.

Wilderness protection on national park and forest land in the Southeast is coming at an agonizingly slow pace. The East has most of the country's population centers. At the same time, it has the least wilderness in terms of numbers of units and acres. Our government is doing a poor job of protecting the little bits and pieces of wilderness we have left.

The Wilderness Act needs to be accorded a fairer interpretation. And protection must be extended to all de facto wilderness in federal ownership. Finally, we need prompt compliance with the law as it is now written. Our conservation efforts will have greater impact on individual wilderness campaigns if we can secure a proper overall interpretation of the present law, coupled with a strong executive order to give all wilderness a chance for protection and preservation.

II.
Working Under
the Wilderness Act

How to Make a Wilderness Study

By Michael McCloskey

If you are interested in making a wilderness study for purposes of developing a wilderness area proposal, it is assumed that you have some understanding of the Wilderness Act, its purposes, procedures and constraints. You must also have some understanding of wilderness values and an appreciation of them. Further, you must have a general knowledge of where undeveloped terrain is located in the region of interest to you.

A wilderness study basically involves two types of work: research in published data, and field work. Research in published data involves collecting and interpreting data from many sources, such as libraries, agencies and interviews. Useful skills include library research techniques, knowledge of governmental organization and the division of responsibilities among agencies, familiarity with basic concepts in many resource development fields, map making and reading, and photo interpretation.

Field work requires not only basic skills in living and moving outdoors, but also sensitivity to wilderness values, imagination in visualizing different management plans, skills in terrain interpretation and map reading.

Basically, there are three general phases in a wilderness study: the *reconnaissance phase*, where one reconnoiters the general area of interest through research and field work to determine which precise area shall be studied in detail as a possible wilderness area; the *resource conflict study phase*, where as much data as possible is accumulated through research concerning the various conflicting resources which exist in the area; and the *boundary selection phase*, where, through field work, wilderness values are positively identified and precise boundaries are picked to protect them.

In accomplishing each phase of a wilderness study, a number of detailed steps must be followed.

Reconnaissance

Three types of federal holdings are subject to the Wilderness Act: parts of the national forests, units of the National Park System (including national parks, national monuments, national seashores and national recreation areas), and wildlife refuges and ranges (under the Bureau of Sport Fisheries and Wildlife). Moreover, the holdings of the Bureau of Land Management can also be zoned for wilderness use under a different law and may also at some time be proposed for inclusion in the Wilderness System.

On the basis of your general experience and interest, examine maps showing the holdings of these agencies to identify remote and undeveloped areas. Pick the particular undeveloped area you wish to study and spot check a few points in it by taking a field trip to verify that it is undeveloped and has wilderness values which should be preserved.

Having determined which general area you want to study, obtain the most detailed and recent maps you can, showing the location of roads of all classes, railroads, and other access facilities (except trails).

Drive to the end of every passable road, and walk to its terminus if it becomes impassable, to verify its exact location, and plot this carefully on a large-scale map. (Logging roads and other roads will frequently extend farther than even the most recent maps show.) Record information on the standards of the road in its last few miles, and information describing development at the roadhead. Also, verify the existence of all other access facilities shown on maps.

Prepare a composite map showing the entire verified road net which delimits the wilderness area. If some roads are so primitive that they could be closed and could revert to nature, show this by a distinguishing symbol. Also, show other access facilities or developments that limit the wilderness quality.

If possible, plot the pattern of road development on a topographical map so that its relationship to land forms may be clearly studied. Locate the large contiguous blocks of roadless country, particularly those that contain entire land forms such as hill or mountain masses, basins and prairies, valleys, canyons or upper drainages.

Choose the largest roadless units, with topographical unity, as the areas you plan to study intensively. Through symbols on your study maps, clearly label the outer boundaries of your study area.

Resource Conflict Study

While presumably the area you have now identified is roadless, it may have been subjected to development and impact in a variety of ways in the past. You must inventory existing developments and uses of the area. From published data (to be supplemented later by field work), compile the following types of data and plot it on your topographical map:

(1) Private rights and ownership: plot the general locations of private inholdings (whether homesteads, railroad grants, or patented or unpatented mining claims; the latter may not be completely recorded, though they may appear on the county tax rolls). From the administering agency and others, determine what licenses or permits have been granted in the area (including licenses to construct dams, grazing permits and packers' permits). Vested private rights are expressly exempted from the management restrictions of the Wilderness Act, but there must not be so many private developments that the area no longer appears *generally* to be wilderness.

(2) Physical disturbance: from specialized maps, reports, records and aerial photographs (if available), determine which places historically have been logged (selectively or clear-cut), mined (locate adits, tailings, placer rubble, and other remains), cultivated (crops or orchards), and grazed (look for present evidence of overgrazing, particularly). This information is necessary to assess whether the area or parts of it still appear to have been affected primarily by the forces of nature. Determine, if possible, what recovery has occurred in disturbed areas.

(3) Structures: from maps and other sources plot the

location of existing buildings, lookouts, heavy-duty bridges and dams. Determine whether the structure is privately owned or licensed or is a public facility (if privately owned, it may be included in a wilderness area). If publicly owned, the facility must be necessary for administering the wilderness area if its continuance is to be allowed.

(4) Installations: locate old road and railroad routes to see whether they have indeed been abandoned and can revert sufficiently. Inventory other communication facilities and utilities that may presently exist in the area: power and telephone lines, flumes, pipelines, landing fields, ski lifts and relay stations. As with structures, these installations may or may not be a bar to wilderness classification, depending on their ownership and purpose.

(4) Use patterns: on the basis of the information above, and on historical records, study reports of the administering agency and estimates of recreational use, develop an understanding of the present patterns of use in the area. Identify zones that have received the heaviest and lightest impact, as well as changing trends in use. Determine particularly which trails, if any, are closed to motorized vehicles, and whether cross-country vehicular traffic is controlled, as well as use by motorboats, float planes and snow vehicles. What are the current pressures from vehicular use?

In the precise study area that has been chosen, develop as much information as possible about *alternative proposals for future development*, so that you know what kinds of conflicts your proposal may encounter. This information is primarily important for Forest Service and Bureau of Land Management holdings. Wildlife refuges are closed to some commercial developments, but not all. Most national park units are closed to all but road, recreational and concessionaire improvements and developments. Many different agencies, in addition to the administering one, have such information in their files.

Obtain information concerning *consumptive resources* in your area of study:

Timber resource. Obtain timber-type maps (from the Forest Service or a state forestry agency) to show existing stands (including such information as species composition, age, density and volume) so that you know which timber may be coveted by lumbermen. If you can, find out whether the timber has been included in the agency's allowable cut and if it has been scheduled for cutting. It is also useful to obtain site and soil vegetation maps to learn whether areas that now support little timber are capable of growing it in the future.

Mineral resource. From the U.S. Geological Survey or a state mineral development agency, obtain maps showing areas of past mineral development, including exact locations of mining prospects. From geological maps, determine locations of formations that hold other areas of possible mineralization. Look at both metallic and nonmetallic minerals, including valuable common minerals, oil, gas, potash, construction materials and geothermal resources (underground steam). Find out anything you can about current private development schemes and prospecting activity.

Forage resource. From the administering agency, find out whether any grazing allotments for cattle, sheep or pack stock exist in the area, and if so, how many AUMs (animal units per month) are involved and whether the allotment is now being used under a permit. If so, how long do the permits run, and is any program underway to reduce grazing? What is the condition of the range, and what is its carrying capacity? Is a rehabilitation program planned? Although some grazing is allowable under the Wilderness Act, the present practice of a permittee, or the management plan of the agency, may conflict with wilderness classification. For instance, what kind of stock-watering facilities and drift fences are installed, and are vehicles used in tending the herd?

Water resource. From various water development agencies (Army Corps of Engineers, Bureau of Reclamation, Soil Conservation Service, as well as comparable state agencies and local power, irrigation and flood control districts, municipal water supply agencies and private utilities), find out whether any water development projects are planned in the area, or whether possible sites have been inventoried. Projects may include hydroelectric developments (dams, pumped storage projects, and diversion structures with tunnels), irrigation developments (both new impoundments and dams raising levels of natural lakes), flood control impoundments and impoundments to augment low flows for navigation, wildlife or pollution-abatement purposes. In some cases, too, impoundments may be proposed to provide reservoir recreation with a warm-water fishery. Where definite proposals have been made, plot on your topographical map the location of the pool to be formed by the impoundments. In many cases, possible projects may conflict. Investigate conflicts, alternatives and the competitive position of agencies proposing conflicting projects. Determine whether any projects have actually been authorized by Congress or licensed by federal authorities such as the Federal Power Commission or comparable state authorities. In some cases, you may want to know what water rights have been established on streams subject to such proposals.

Wildlife resource. While wilderness classification protects the habitat for many types of rare and endangered and other species, it can conflict with plans of wildlife agencies to manage an area to favor certain preferred game species. From the state game agency and the administering agency procure information about game populations, trends and problems. Determine whether any problem of securing sufficient hunter access for proper levels of stocking is reported, and evaluate the problem. Roads may be proposed to improve access, or demands made for access by motorboat, float plane, helicopter, snow or trail vehicle. Study the winter range problem also to see whether wilderness status might serve to protect the range. Where conflicts with wilderness classification are apparent, form a judgment about which species would be benefited by contrasting management and which would be preferred and what the result of decreased management would be.

Obtain information concerning *construction proposals* in your area of study:

Transportation. Investigate possible schemes for installing transportation facilities in the area, including highways (interstate, state, county or forest), railroads, monorails, tramways, tunnels, landing fields and canals. Check particularly the list of authorized state highways, county roads and transportation system maps of the administering agency.

Utilities. From public utilities, such as power companies, telephone companies, water supply agencies, gas companies and aviation agencies, find out whether they have plans for running power lines, telephone lines, flumes or pipelines through the area. Beacons, radar stations and relay stations may also be contemplated.

Recreational facilities. Among the facilities incompatible with wilderness classification are ski resorts with lodges and lifts, hunting cabins, packers' stations with highly developed loading platforms, corrals and sheds, developed campgrounds, and boat-launching ramps. The recreational planners of the administering agency may be planning such facilities, often in cooperation with a permittee. State and regional development agencies are frequently involved, too, in promoting such facilities (with inventories, for instance, of possible winter sports development sites). Shelters are allowed in wilderness areas only if needed for the health and safety of users.

Scientific apparatus. Universities and research agencies are increasingly interested in installing observatories, research stations and various monitoring and measuring devices in remote and high areas. While research is an intended purpose of wilderness areas, the means with which it is pursued must be compatible with the quality of wilderness; e.g., observation plots, collection devices and small recording instruments. Buildings, conspicuous equipment and physical manipulation of the environment are incompatible.

Administrative facilities. The Wilderness Act allows in wilderness areas only those administrative facilities that are essential for administering the classified areas. Facilities existing to serve purposes outside the wilderness or merely adding to the comfort and convenience of users are not allowed. Thus, bridges, lookouts and guard stations may or may not be allowable in wilderness areas, depending on their purpose. Look at the fire plan for the area to determine whether any permanent fire roads are planned. While temporary fire roads are allowed in wilderness areas, permanent ones are not.

Boundary Selection

Once all of this data has been compiled and analyzed, you will be ready to determine the boundaries of your wilderness proposal through map studies and field work.

Transfer pertinent data already compiled onto maps suitable for field use. Generally a topographical map will be most suitable as a base map, but often the cultural data on it is out of date. Cultural data is likely to be most up to date on maps being used locally by the administering agency. Consolidate all data, if possible, on an overall planning map, and if necessary onto larger-scale maps for different sectors that will be visited. Check for discrepancies and inaccuracies between maps; early maps may vary considerably with respect to survey lines, topography and culture. Because of their remoteness, areas of wilderness quality are often the last to have up-to-date maps.

It is advisable to let the local office of the administering agency know about your travel plans, both as a courtesy and safety measure and to obtain more accurate, detailed information. Usually it will not be desirable to accept a guided tour by that office, but it may be helpful for them to tie in a visit to your party in the field. If this does not occur, you may want to visit the office again after the trip to obtain answers to questions prompted by your field observations.

In order to develop a travel plan for your field work, first develop a list of priorities in what you want to visit.

Provide time to sample the core of unfamiliar sectors, to
study the problem areas and to pick boundaries. Areas
where resource conflicts have already been identified
should probably get the most attention. Be flexible
enough, however, to change your priorities as you progress if new opportunities are suggested by what you
see. In many cases you will find you need to plan additional ground surveys.

In terms of your time, manpower, skill and financing,
develop a travel plan most likely to cover your priorities. Determine whether horses would extend your range
or merely be a costly encumbrance. Plan a route, wherever possible, to avoid doubling back. By map inspection, try to identify promontories as destinations which
will afford the best views into zones that must be in-
spected.

Visit the component topographical units within the
general study area to verify their wilderness quality. It
may not be necessary to study each in detail. If time is
limited, a peripheral penetration or view into them may
be sufficient to verify that the country is indeed wilderness.

The value of a potential wilderness area should be
judged in terms of the degree to which it possesses the
following qualities: (1) wildness (lack of the marks of
man); (2) remoteness (sense of distance from civilization); (3) seclusion (masked from views of developments); (4) ecological stability (tendency toward climax
flora); (5) opportunity and challenge for wilderness
skills (hiking, riding, backpacking, mountaineering, river
running, nature study, pack-hunting, fly-fishing, etc.);
(6) opportunity to observe native wildlife; (7) awesome
or scenic landscapes; (8) intrinsic relationship to other

wilderness units—topographically, ecologically, visually, or in terms of recreational use patterns; (9) capacity to recover natural appearance, if presently disturbed.

If the study area has any present type of protective classification, locate that boundary on the ground and assess its adequacy. Consider the desirability of expansion.

Visit each locality with a resource conflict problem and weigh the value of the area as wilderness against its probable value if put to a nonwilderness use. Try to visualize the effect of resource development. If already developed, try to visualize the possibilities for the area if the developments were removed, and the problems were complicated. Where a number of related developments could take place, assess the impact of likely combinations of them. Explore alternatives for development beyond the wilderness study area.

Once it is determined that wilderness classification is the highest value for a unit, draw general schematic boundaries around the unit on the planning map. Develop a composite map showing the aggregate of such units.

Locate features on the ground that can be positively identified to which boundaries can be tied in order to secure maximum protection for each unit to be protected as wilderness. If a hill mass is to be protected, do not cut it down the middle with a ridge-line boundary. If a drainage, however, is to be protected, a ridge line may be the best boundary line. In choosing boundaries, distinguish between the object of protection and the problems of selecting boundaries to protect it. While a boundary should be readily identifiable and easily administered, the object of protection should not be sacrificed in order to find an easily identifiable feature. Depending on circumstances, such things as topographical features, legally surveyed section lines (and subdivisions of them) and metes and bounds may all serve satisfactorily as boundaries. Where the topography runs at right angles to the boundary direction, topographical features may not prove to be feasible boundary markers. Where possible, pick a boundary line that can be checked while still in the field.

Plot the successive legs of your boundary on your master planning map. Label each leg with a letter or number keyed to a report that you should write explaining why each unit should be protected as wilderness and why the particular boundary location was chosen. Boundary legs should be chosen with an eye both to the unit needing protection and to the connections that must be made with adjoining legs. Where boundaries have legs based on surveyed lines or metes and bounds, or where maps are poor, a written boundary description may be needed. The more specific and well-reasoned a boundary recommendation for a wilderness area, the more helpful and persuasive it will prove to be with the agencies that receive it.

On the basis of the foregoing study and field work, a proposal report should be prepared, including the following information: (1) Introduction, giving the purpose of the report and a summary including the protection proposed, location and acreage; (2) General findings, including the value of each wilderness area, a description of it and justification of boundaries suggested; and (3) Maps and references.

Organizing Support for a Wilderness Proposal

By Michael McCloskey

Under the Wilderness Act a proposal to include an area in the National Wilderness Preservation System is drawn up by the administering federal agency. In the case of de facto wilderness (for which no reviews are required under the Wilderness Act), if the agency has no plans to propose that an area be included in the Wilderness System, conservationists must draw up their own proposal, seek congressional sponsors for it and work for its passage through Congress in order to preserve the area as part of the Wilderness System. The following guidelines on organizing support for a wilderness proposal are mainly for working under the terms set down in the Wilderness Act, although in general they apply to organizing support for de facto wilderness proposals.

Types of Support Needed

Support of the administering agency is most important because this agency has the greatest influence in shaping the proposal that will go before Congress. You will have opportunities to influence the agency's recommendations in four phases: (1) By making advance inquiries at the time you are shaping your own proposal (see "How to Make a Wilderness Study"). (2) By submitting your own written proposal to the agency for consideration. In some cases you may want to publicize this event in order to build public awareness and support for your proposal. If this is done when the agency begins its own wilderness study, it could encourage a continuing dialogue between you and your supporters and agency personnel. (3) Public hearings afford the most conspicuous and critical opportunity to participate in the process of policy formation. Under the Wilderness Act two types of hearings take place. *Administrative hearings* are held in the locality nearest the wilderness in question in order to gather public reaction to the administering agency's proposal. *Legislative hearings* are held by Congress after receiving a wilderness proposal from the executive branch. Such hearings customarily are held in Washington, D.C., before the Committees on Interior and Insular Affairs, but in some cases field hearings may also be held, especially in the case of controversial proposals. Each house of Congress holds at least one hearing on each proposal. When proposals fail to pass one Congress, they may again be subject to a hearing in succeeding Congresses. (More information on techniques of organizing a presentation at a hearing will follow.) (4) Following a hearing it is often appropriate to inquire further about the agencies' plans. Agencies are expected to reconsider their proposals in the light of public comment at the hearing. If the testimony is largely adverse to the agency proposal, changes of some sort often ensue. You should keep in touch with agency personnel working on revisions and the hearing record, both to further influence the revisions and to be prepared for changes.

Support of other public officials can be valuable. Under the Wilderness Act, state governors, county officials and other affected federal agencies are invited to offer commentaries on wilderness proposals. You should contact these officials in advance of hearings to develop an understanding of their point of view, and hopefully their support.

Support from other organizations (conservation and nonconservation oriented) is important because it can involve large numbers of people in your case and because group names have a built-in recognition value with the public. Although the support of conservation groups is often expected, if some fail to go on the record, it may be noticed—their absence may suggest a division in the ranks of conservationists. Support from nonconservation groups is particularly important in showing a broad spectrum of interest in a wilderness proposal. Approach civic, service, business, farm and labor organizations to solicit their support. These groups often are involved deeply in the political structure of small communities.

The Congress and the administering agencies traditionally are disproportionately responsive to the opinion of local residents in land management controversies. For this reason, *support within local communities* is very important. Time invested in making friends in communities near the wilderness can be most rewarding. Packers, guides or local sportsmen's clubs may provide an entrée into such communities. Local residents may know very little about formal wilderness area classification procedures. While they may approve keeping the area just the way it is now, they may be hostile to any proposal they do not understand. Advance education may prevent a fire of opposition from ever starting. With frequent ties to commodity industries, however, these communities will usually have some individuals opposed to wilderness classification.

You should seek *support of the press*, for you must depend heavily on it in your efforts to reach a large audience. Editorial page editors and outdoor column writers will usually be interested in wilderness proposals. Because these writers are often influential in small communities, it is important to acquaint them with your proposal and keep them abreast of developments. Even those who are not sympathetic initially will appreciate being kept informed. Do not neglect local television or radio stations. Through national conservation organizations, or other contacts you may have, try to promote coverage in regional and national publications.

In the final analysis, the success of your wilderness proposal will depend on *support from individuals*. Do not be afraid to start with just one or two persons. They in turn can recruit more. Constitute yourselves as an ad hoc committee. When your viewpoint is reported in the press more people will let you know they share your opinion. Get as many of these people as possible to attend the hearings on the proposal, and urge them to speak out—and to keep writing to their elected officials.

The Nature of a Public Hearing

History. The public hearing is probably descended from the ancient tradition of the royal audience mentioned in biblical times. Today the government proposes and the citizen voices opinions of approval or disapproval, whereas in the royal audience the citizen or subject proposed a favor and the monarch approved or disapproved. The Anglo-American adversary system of justice has set a standard of fairness requiring that both sides of an argument be fully heard which has carried over into legislative and administrative branches of government. But the traditions requiring that both sides of an issue be heard date from early times in deliberative assemblies. More than 1,900 years ago the Roman, Seneca, said, "He who decides a case without hearing the other side . . . even though he decides justly, cannot be considered just."

Types of hearings. Hearings held by branches of government include those held by committees of legislative bodies, administrative bodies and regulatory bodies. Committees of legislative bodies that hold hearings are those of the Congress, state legislatures and city councils. Characteristics of these hearings are: a panel presiding, with chairman; questioning of controversial witnesses; and overt references to political philosophies.

Administrative bodies that hold hearings include the Forest Service, the National Park Service, state water resources boards and county planning commissions. Characteristics of these hearings are: usually a single hearing officer presiding, an attorney at federal hearings, although a panel may preside with a chairman at some state hearings; an aura of professional impartiality commonly presented, with little questioning of witnesses except to clarify factual questions as to the meaning of a viewpoint; oaths occasionally administered, especially at the state level.

Regulatory bodies that hold hearings include bodies with quasi-judicial authority such as the Federal Power Commission and state public utility commissions. Characteristics of these hearings are: either a single examiner presiding, an attorney employed by the body or the commission, or members of it; oaths sometimes administered and witnesses not only questioned but possibly cross-examined by attorneys for the opposing side; many procedures judicial in nature; testimony restricted to strictly defined questions often technical in nature.

Generally, the most formality and development of procedure is found in hearings of regulatory bodies; less before legislative bodies and the least before administrative bodies. This is primarily true within any one level of government but is not true between levels of government. Conceptual sophistication seems greatest with administrative bodies, less with regulatory, and the least with legislative bodies.

The greatest formality, and procedural and conceptual sophistication is usually found in hearings before federal agencies; less before state agencies; and the least before hearings of bodies of local government (city, county, special districts). Arguments must be adjusted to account for these differences. Personal contact with the deciding officer is most important at the local level (more important than the merits of the argument), whereas at higher levels it is likely to be ineffective, harmful, or even illegal (before federal regulatory agencies).

Functions of the hearing. Hearings have a legal as well as political function. Legally, the hearing is a formal method of public consultation in the making of laws, policies or regulations. (Other methods of consultation include soliciting written public comment by public notice, advisory boards and study commissions.) Of course, informal methods of public consultation (office conferences, etc.) are used also and can supplement the formal methods.

The political function of the hearing should be understood from the agency's viewpoint as well as the viewpoint of the potential witness. An agency may hold a *hearing to promote a substantive policy*: to gather public reactions to it, especially favorable ones; to test its political feasibility; to offer an opportunity to clear up misunderstandings about it; or to discredit opposing policies through manipulating the scenario at the hearing. For example, an agency's decision may actually be predetermined, and the hearing held as a political necessity merely to give an appearance of fairness. (This is common before legislative bodies and at local levels.)

An agency may hold a *hearing to determine the need for a policy or the value of one proposed*. In this instance, the agency may have a sincere desire to gather information and a cross-section of viewpoints and evaluations with respect to the effects of the policy proposed. Here the decision is not predetermined.

An agency may also hold a *hearing to improve its own political position*—by accommodating itself to the prevailing attitude; by shifting the focus of pressure from itself to the interacting contestants who are provided with a forum to confront each other; by providing a vehicle for adjusting intergroup differences through the drama therapy of a hearing; by gaining publicity for itself, its members or chairman; or by satisfying political obligations to those who want a hearing at a given time or place. In these instances, the decision may *not* be predetermined, or even regarded as important. Or it may never be made at all.

From the viewpoint of the potential witness, the hearing may be regarded as an occasion for advancing a cause on its merits by persuasive argument, and as an opportunity to develop an idea before a significant audience and to secure added exposure for it. Also, it is an occasion for influencing decision-making by a show of political force where public opinion is organized and brought to bear at the most public and politically sensitive moment.

Evaluation of a hearing. Both the decision-makers and the public evaluate a hearing.

Later the decision-makers usually prepare two documents about the hearing. The first is a transcript or record of testimony presented, often a verbatim account. It is often analyzed as follows: (1) the main lines of argument for different positions are identified and listed; (2) the number of witnesses supporting each main line of argument are counted and recorded; (3) a listing of represented organizations is developed by their size and importance. The second document usually prepared is a report of recommendations to a higher body having final authority. It is prepared by the hearing officer, an examiner or a committee. Sometimes, however, a hearing officer at administrative hearings does not make recommendations but merely presides. He may, though, submit a short report of his impressions of the oral testimony.

The public evaluates a hearing through press reports which often characterize the impact of the hearing and suggest which side made the more persuasive case. Additionally, groups that testified may circulate reports on the outcome of the hearing, either claiming that the hearing has demonstrated that greater support exists for its position and that the validity of its viewpoint has been established, or offering some explanation for its poor showing. The agency that held the hearing may also circulate accounts of the hearing seeking to prove that its policies may have been vindicated by a show of public support. These accounts are sometimes highly inaccurate.

Testifying at a Hearing

The amount of preparation you make for a public hearing, and the nature of it, will be determined by the kind of hearing, the importance of the issue, the amount of controversy and the time and resources available to your forces.

General determinations. From your position on the issue, determine the strategy of your presentation before the hearing. *If the desired decision is maintenance of the status quo*, and the hearing agency is suspected of favoring this, then make a dispassionate, factual presentation. The numbers of witnesses for your side will probably be more important than elaborate development of your arguments. If the agency favors change, however, then arguments are most important and a less restrained approach is indicated.

If the desired decision involves a change in policy or practice, then it is most important to have a large number of witnesses, and that you outnumber your opponents. Presentations should be restrained in tone if your position is well known and understood, if the change is not an unusual one, and if the agency favors the change or is neutral. If your position is not well understood and is unappreciated, then the quality of your arguments is most important, although numbers help, too. Arguments should be varied, both simple and complex, and colorful. But be careful never consciously to misstate a fact because this will jeopardize your credibility. Do adequate research beforehand.

If the desired decision is most unlikely to be forthcoming, and evidence exists that the issue has been predetermined, then an alternative strategy can sometimes be adopted if there is a factual basis for it. This consists of bringing pressure to bear on the agency by trying to embarrass or discredit it through challenging the impartiality of the forum—for instance, citing evidence that the decision has begun to be implemented before the hearing, or that the scope of the issue at the hearing has been unfairly limited, or that the questioning is biased or harassing. Such charges will invite close questioning, as will exaggerated or patently inaccurate charges.

Determine which potential audiences you are addressing. If you intend mainly to address decision-makers in the agency either through the record or through the presiding officer, then dispassionate statements with factual content may make the best impression. If impressions of the hearing officer are important, it is important to testify early, while he is more attentive.

If you mean primarily to address the public at large, as reached through the press (newspapers, radio or television), then simplified, colorful statements are most effective. Early presentation is also essential because of both the limited attention span of reporters, and midday deadlines of the many newspapers printing afternoon editions.

If you mean to address specialized audiences, including those present (e.g., your opponents or your own adherents), then the psychological reaction of the crowd may be important in affecting representatives of the agency and the press. You may also want to rally your own forces with your statement, or challenge your opponents (while perhaps wanting to conceal things from them). The tone of presentation should depend on your aim.

Determine which type of statement you are to make. You may be more impressive if you can speak for the numbers represented by an organization rather than just yourself. If so, mention the size of the membership of the organization if it is large or significant, and always be prepared to answer questions about the size and geographical distribution of the membership as well as its purposes. In speaking for organizations, you are usually limited in content by an authorizing resolution adopted by them. If so, refer to it by date and place in your presentation to make your authority clear. Authorization to testify on behalf of an organization will usually require that arrangements be made well in advance of the hearing; e.g., as much as a year or more to secure a suitable resolution from an annual convention. Attempt to secure advantageous resolutions and presentations from as diverse a spread of organizations as possible; don't be content with bringing out only the organizations in your traditional alliance of interest groups. (But make sure they are all there. If any are missing, it may be inferred that there is dissension in your ranks and that the alliance is breaking up.)

If you are making a personal statement, you have the advantage of flexibility in the scope and style of your presentation. Personal statements are not dependent on the set content of a resolution and can be adjusted to the development of the arguments. Individuals making such statements should usually avoid indicating membership in organizations for which others are testifying, so as to avoid any inference that the organizations may be getting additional opportunities to be heard. Nevertheless, do not conceal membership if asked.

Determine the argumentative emphasis you wish to make. A few able individuals should present the basic arguments, dividing up the subject matter if time is limited. These persons should testify close together in order of appearance so as to maintain unity in the argument. Oral summaries may be given, but complete statements should be submitted for the record. Usually representatives of the main interested organizations will want to present these basic arguments.

Support for arguments previously stated merely adds the weight of numbers to the record. If time is limited, witnesses should not hesitate to summarize presentations. However, it is most important that they indicate clearly which substantive position they support. They should not assume that the agency will be able to infer it. Supporting witnesses should always follow the witnesses giving basic arguments.

Rebuttal statements can be either anticipatory or responsive. If the arguments of your opposition are regarded as damaging and likely to be well presented, it may be wise to anticipate them by having an able witness rebut them early in the hearing. If it is unclear as to whether these arguments will appear, it may be well to avoid giving them undue emphasis by advance rebuttal; you may want to wait until near the end when an appraisal can be made. An able witness can be held in reserve for that time to rebut whichever opposition arguments appear most damaging. If an able witness has not been held in reserve, determine whether a witness still to be called can yield his time to a more able witness who has already testified, or to one who has not been scheduled. Also, an able witness can request in advance that his speaking time be divided, so as to save some of it for rebuttal at the end of the hearing.

The *tone* of your statement will depend upon whom you are addressing and the point you wish to make. Keep a dispassionate tone when the agency is your primary audience and it is receptive to your line of argument. It is useful to adopt a provocative tone when you desire to attract attention and your views are otherwise likely to be neglected. A provocative tone is also recommended if you wish to worry apathetic and unsympathetic audiences.

A colorfully quotable tone is best for the public at large; the press is most likely to use such passages. These presentations should be specifically planned, with press releases distributed in advance of your presentation as well as at the hearing.

Determine your mode of presentation. A *written statement* is required before congressional hearings (see House of Representatives Rule XI, par. 25 [f]) and some other hearings, although this rule is not always enforced. Oral testimony without any supporting written statement is often accepted at congressional hearings in the field. Between twenty-five and fifty copies of written statements are usually required for presentation to a congressional committee, though fewer are needed if your statement is merely submitted for the record without being read aloud. Multiple copies are intended for each member of the panel plus the press. Copies are often scanned in their entirety while the witness reads part of it; questions may then be asked relating to parts not read aloud.

Written statements facilitate accurate expression of your views for the record, and help quiet nervousness. They have the drawback, however, of being less easy to condense when time is limited. They also make less of an impact on the audience present, and cannot be adapted to relate to preceding testimony. To facilitate possible condensation, organize them in pyramid form (as are newspaper articles), with all of the essential material in the opening paragraphs and elaborating material following. Additionally, organize them so you are able to stop reading after one minute, two minutes, five minutes or ten minutes' time has elapsed.

Oral statements (without a written statement for submission) can be either prepared (with or without notes) or extemporaneous. If well done, they can make the greatest impact on the audience, including the hearing officer, but this may not be important if he is just a presiding officer and does not make recommendations. Such testimony, however, often appears disjointed and awkward and even misleading in the hearing record, and the record may be the most important consideration. Therefore oral statements at a formal hearing should be attempted only by able public speakers. If the hearing is informal and no transcript is being compiled, an oral statement may be preferable.

Through a *combination* of an oral summary of less important parts of a written statement and a reading of key parts where the wording must be exact, you can develop a flexible approach which can be adjusted to fit limitations of time.

Questioning occurs mainly in legislative and regulatory hearings, usually with only perfunctory questioning in administrative hearings. When leading questions are asked, do not assent to oversimplified premises. Avoid definite answers in cases where you are doubtful about how to respond. Request permission to provide a more adequate answer in writing at a later time.

Determine ahead of time whether props will be helpful. Find out whether *maps* will be furnished or, if needed, whether you should furnish them. Determine whether you can submit maps for the record and whether they can be folded. In referring to points on maps during the testimony, mention the points by name so that your testimony is complete in the record.

Only black and white *photographs* can be printed in the record, although color photos may be included in the file. Copies of photos should be available for display to the hearing panel. On rare occasions *slides* can be shown, though nothing appears in the record unless black and white prints are made. Speed in setting up the showing is essential, as well as great selectivity in what is shown (ordinarily, less than a dozen are allowed).

Articles and *reprints* can often accompany testimony, but a request that they be printed in the record will not always be granted. If they are long or numerous, they are likely just to be placed in the file. *Letters* from persons who could not be present and stacks of *petitions* can be presented to the hearing officer. You should arrange for publicity on petitions, particularly. *Room displays* with literature for distribution will sometimes be allowed. Make advance arrangements for such a display.

Specific procedures. Note carefully vital information in the initial announcement of the hearing. The following physical details should be noted: (1) hearing *date* (determine how much organizing time you have until that date); (2) *place* (often a hostile agency will schedule the hearing at a place advantageous to its witnesses, where your forces are thin); (3) *length* (an all-day hearing will usually last only six hours, during which time about fifty to sixty witnesses can be processed if an average speaking time of about five minutes per person is allowed); (4) *opening hour* (plan to arrive thirty minutes early); (5) name of *presiding officer or membership of presiding panel* (determine backgrounds to gauge strategy); (6) name of *whom to contact* for further information.

Note the *scope of issues* to which testimony will be limited. A rule of germaneness is enforced to some extent in almost all hearings—least so in administrative hearings and most so in regulatory hearings. Legislative hearings vary a great deal according to the political factors involved.

Also note the method of requesting to be called as a witness, and the deadline for submitting such requests. (Congressional hearings often specify a deadline as much as ten days in advance of the hearing date.) If no method is specified, it is safe to submit a request by mail.

Determine how widely the hearing announcement has been disseminated. Perhaps you should disseminate it more widely to your allies.

Organization of witnesses. Form a committee to coordinate arrangements for your forces at the hearing. An existing organization may be able to furnish an apparatus to serve this function, or it may be desirable to form a special ad hoc committee for an alliance of forces. The more time available to accomplish this, the better. The committee should select an advance coordinator and a floor leader for the day of the hearing. Usually the committee will want to encourage as large a turnout of its forces as possible, but occasionally this may not be desirable, as at hearings of local government units, which can become chaotic. The committee thus will usually send a mailer to its adherents encouraging attendance and testimony, and will follow up by telephoning prospective witnesses to persuade them to testify.

The committee should determine the minimum number of witnesses needed to counterbalance the opposition in the time available and should make sure that at least that number is present. (In an all-day hearing, you will probably need thirty-five witnesses to be assured of a majority.) A checklist of expected witnesses should be prepared and double-checked. The day prior to the hearing, it is often desirable to gain a publicity advantage by distributing a press release of the testimony your leading organizations plan to present at the hearing. Also, arrangements should be made if there will be special opportunities for advantageous publicity at the hearing itself.

Scheduling of witnesses. The most common methods of calling witnesses are designed to be simple, mechanical and fair to all sides. Usually, however, they do not facilitate the orderly exposition of arguments. Witnesses may be called to testify in a chronological order by date of receipt of mailed requests, or by the order in which they sign registration cards prior to the opening of the hearing. Sometimes a combination of these methods is used. Or witnesses may be called alphabetically by last names. Alternating witnesses from various sides may be called one after the other, or blocks of time assigned to various sides (half-hour, one hour or half-day) may be alternated. In this case, the issue must be susceptible to being easily divided into a limited number of sides, and witnesses are required to indicate their sides in registering. The respective sides may also be asked to submit lists of their witnesses.

A *three-fold order of priority* is used for administrative hearings under the Wilderness Act. Public officials speak first, organizations second, and individuals third, with priority given to those who can testify only at a given time or those who have come the greatest distance. Other individuals may then be called in any of the three ways just mentioned, with the alphabetical order being followed in most cases.

When you register as a witness, mail in your request to testify as quickly as possible upon receipt of the hearing notice, especially when testifying on behalf of organizations. Find out if the methods for calling witnesses have been decided. It is most important to have your basic arguments and quotable statements presented early, while the press and panel are attentive, and to avoid losing your best witnesses who, if they have to wait a long time, may have to leave before they can testify. If the methods have not been decided, your hearing coordinator should suggest to the agency the method that will be most advantageous. If your requests have been submitted very early, the chronological method may be best. If many of your best witnesses have last names with initials early in the alphabet, then the alphabetical method may be best. If you have a number of public officials on your side and also many organizations, then the three-fold order system may be best. If your forces are weak in comparison to the opposition, the alternating method may be best.

In requesting that a particular method of scheduling be adopted, emphasize the need for an orderly, fair one which can be known well in advance. If no commitments are made with respect to methods of calling witnesses, ask your key witnesses to request to testify early, particularly if that is the only time they can be available for it.

On the *day of the hearing* arrive at least thirty minutes early to sign registration cards, in case witnesses are called by that method. If no method for calling witnesses has yet been announced, the floor leader should approach the presiding officer and propose an advantageous method. The floor leader should also learn from the presiding officer whether witnesses can yield their time and position on the witness list to others, and whether witnesses can divide their allotted time.

Conduct during the hearing. Before you testify try to determine your position on the witness list, either from your floor leader or the clerk. Be sure to be present at the time when your name is to be called. After you testify, stay as long as possible in order to counterbalance the physical presence of the opposition. (Although applause is usually not allowed, it is sometimes tolerated. If it is, your side should not be underrepresented.)

After you testify, pass a copy of your statement, if you have one, to the press table, if the floor leader has not already done so. Be available for interviews on radio or television. Find out whether your forces are holding a post-mortem session after the hearing. If so, attend.

Duties of the *floor leader* at this time include: informing witnesses of when they can expect to be called; reminding them just before they are called, and of about how much time they will have for their testimony; assisting them in condensing their statements to fit the time allotted; answering for missing witnesses, explaining whether they will return or not, and submitting statements for the record for those who have had to leave (in submitting each statement, he should state whether the witness is for or against the proposition at issue); and arranging press interviews for quotable witnesses, making sure that the press gets copies of all newsworthy statements benefiting his cause (usually there is a press table for the statements).

Etiquette at a public hearing. The characteristic distinction between administrative and legislative hearings is that in a legislative hearing, the witness is carrying on a face-to-face dialogue with the key decision-makers, whereas this is often not so in an administrative hearing. In the latter, the witness is usually dictating a statement for the written record and for coverage by the press. The decision-makers do not preside. A technical hearing officer does, and merely superintends the process of compiling a transcript of testimony. He does not ask questions of witnesses. Legislators, however, do ask questions. They respond to the manner in which testimony is presented. Further, they react against breaches of etiquette in appearances before them. If conservationists are to make good appearances, they should thoroughly understand the rules of etiquette at a legislative hearing. The premise behind these rules is the need for fair and expeditious procedure and for controls over the verbal combat of contestants in a dramatic and emotionally charged setting. The controls also reinforce the authority and dialectical advantage of the presiding panel. As a witness you should *never* forget that the panel is running the hearing and that the inherent advantage in any exchange of viewpoints is always with the panel. Its members *always* have the last word—*they* are the critical decision-makers.

Rules on testimony. When witness lists are long, be patient with the committee in its difficult struggle to accommodate an unusually large number of speakers. Often it will be necessary to shift the order of witnesses or to take them out of order. Such changes typically are made so that government witnesses can be heard first, and then those witnesses who must leave early.

If you request to testify at a given time because of the pressure of other commitments, be certain that you are present when your name is scheduled to be called. The committee is indulging you as a courtesy when it agrees to call certain witnesses at prescribed times. Do not disregard that courtesy.

Keep brief your introductory remarks that qualify you as a relevant witness. Do not spend more time describing your background on the subject than you do in stating your position. Correctly represent your authority to speak for an organization, if you are doing so. It is often helpful to cite briefly the resolution or directive that authorizes you to speak for a group. If you are not speaking for an organization, do not imply that you are by listing your membership in it, or referring to the offices that you hold, or by wearing its badges or uniforms. Deception of this sort can discredit all of your testimony.

Present only testimony relevant to the issue before the panel. The panel is apt to be annoyed if you spend much time discussing questions that are unrelated to the issue or that are beyond their power to change. A legislative hearing is not an occasion to air all of the grievances you may have on various subjects.

Concentrate on testimony that is new and has not been covered before. Committees rankle at receiving highly repetitious testimony. When the point you planned to make has already been adequately covered, merely say: "Mr. Smith has already ably covered the point I was going to make; nevertheless, he omitted . . ." or "I would like to add . . . ," and in a few words make a further point. If you really have nothing to add, just say: "Mr. Smith has already covered my point perhaps better than I could have. I just wish to say I fully agree with him." The panel will often be behind schedule and will appreciate your helping them to catch up, and may remember your "point" better by this effective reemphasis.

Avoid injecting partisan politics into your remarks. If the panel is nonpartisan, your remarks may be resented by members of both parties. If the panel is partisan in make-up, members of the opposite party can be expected to resent your remarks. You may need the good will of every member of the panel.

Do not engage in name-dropping to emphasize your importance. Let others point out your importance, not yourself. Never refer to social or business connections with a member of the panel. This is especially true before local and administrative boards.

Conclude your testimony when your allotted time expires. In a crowded hearing it is frequently necessary to limit testimony to five minutes or less. Do not insist on running over your time. Never disregard the chairman's request that you conclude. (He may not always object to your finishing your sentence.)

Rules on content. Some additional rules with respect to the substance of your testimony should be observed. Restrict your testimony to matters on which you are competent to testify and on which testimony is needed. Do not pose as an expert on matters that you know little about, and do not lecture the panel on matters on which they may be expert. For instance, do not lecture a legislative committee on national parks about the value of national parks. It is presumptuous to imply that the committee does not know its business.

In presenting your testimony, assume that the committee is deliberating in good faith even if it does not appear to be sympathetic. Do not criticize its performance or impugn its motives. A committee's true motives are hard to know, and such charges can only hurt your standing with it.

Similarly, speak with respect for your opponents. Concede that they may be well motivated and that your differences are probably honest ones. If you are so ungracious as to belittle them, you are only likely to invite a reprimand from the chair. The chairman may suggest that you concentrate on your own case and that the committee will be the judge of the opposition's case.

In concluding, it is a courtesy to thank the panel for allowing you to speak. A simple "Thank you, Mr. Chairman" is often sufficient.

Rules on response. The sternest test of hearing room etiquette may come when a witness is questioned. Close questioning may suggest that the questioner is unfriendly. Searching or leading questions, however, are often used to clarify obscure points and to reveal unstated assumptions. Such questions may or may not indicate that the questioner is hostile. But in any event, the witness can only lose ground in his efforts to be persuasive if he in turn reacts in a hostile manner. These rules should always be followed: (1) Allow the questioner to finish before responding. Do not break in before he has. This is common courtesy. (2) Present your response in a calm and restrained manner. Do not become argumentative or combative. Winning a public argument with a committee member may be the surest way of losing his vote. Do not make the questioner your adversary—he should be instead the object of your persuasive efforts. (3) Be modest and undogmatic in making your response. Defiant or arrogant assertions to the effect that it should be self-evident your position is correct can only turn the committee against you.

Rules for spectators. Even when not testifying, as a member of the audience one should observe certain rules of conduct. Most presiding officers ask the audience to refrain from applauding or otherwise demonstrating its approval or disapproval of statements made by speakers. Unruly audience behavior demeans the dignity of the forum and delays the progress of the hearing. If partisans of a point of view repeatedly disregard the chair's requests, much of the good will that speakers for that point of view have earned will be dissipated.

Finally, partisans of each side should avoid displays of propaganda that are disturbing to the decorum of the hearing room. For example, banners and placards should not be exhibited. Such displays are not allowed in hearings in Washington, D.C., or at state capitols. It is a challenge to the committee's authority to attempt them in the less controlled circumstances of field hearings.

After the hearing. Find out how long the record will be open for the submission of further written statements; these can be either additional supporting statements and supplemental information, or arguments to answer unanswered points raised by the opposition during the hearing. Often the record is left open for ten, fourteen or thirty days. With hearings by local units of government, additional supporting statements may be of less importance, and personal contact more influential. At higher levels, however, such statements are quite important in a negative sense—your cause is not advanced a great deal by having a large majority of witnesses, but it is hurt if you are badly outnumbered. In organizing letter writing campaigns for the record, do not suggest a form letter or even specific wording, because uniformity in the wording of letters will suggest that a campaign has been waged—and letters resulting from a campaign are accorded much less weight than letters that have the earmarks of being spontaneous.

Finally, if an oral statement was presented somewhat unevenly, find out from the presiding officer whether you can edit the proofs before it is printed in the record.

After the Hearing

By Harry B. Crandell

The National Forest Service, National Park Service and Bureau of Sport Fisheries and Wildlife are required to hold public hearings on the results of their field studies of potential wilderness areas under Section 3 (c) of the Wilderness Act. This requirement for public involvement and input into the recommendations of each agency is the first step in what has come to be called the "wilderness review process," which culminates when Congress enacts a law incorporating a wilderness into the National Wilderness Preservation System.

Public hearings are supposed to provide an opportunity for citizen conservationists to express their opinions and thereby influence the decisions of the agencies. Unfortunately, the attitude of most federal agencies

Mr. Crandell is director of wilderness reviews of The Wilderness Society. Formerly he directed the planning and wilderness programs in the National Wildlife Refuge System for the Bureau of Sport Fisheries and Wildlife. These remarks were presented at the Twelfth Biennial Sierra Club Wilderness Conference, in Washington, D.C., on September 24, 1971.

thwarts and frustrates this supposition. The attitude goes something like this: "We're the experts, we are the professionals, and we're managing these areas in the *public interest.* Now then, you, the public, leave us alone and let us run the area in a way that we think is best." This patronizing attitude is most prevalent when citizens don't agree with a proposed action by a federal agency, and it is the rule rather than the exception in the wilderness review process where, more often than not, at a public hearing conservationists do not agree with the wilderness proposal of a federal agency.

I believe conservationists are making a serious mistake in the wilderness review process by not working to influence agency decisions *throughout* the months or even years that the review process is taking place. Conservationists show up at public hearings en masse, make recommendations to the agencies, and expect the agencies to adopt them thereafter. But, why should the agencies adopt them? After all, the agency personnel feel they are the "experts" and are charged with the responsibility of not only interpreting the Wilderness Act to fit their needs but also applying the law to a specific wilderness proposal. Currently, the public hearing record is the document coming from outside the federal government helping to influence agency thought and subsequent decisions.

The wilderness review process, however, is *not* limited to the initial action (the public hearing) or the final action (an act of Congress). These are parts of the whole, and important parts, too. But between the public hearing and congressional determinations another important part of the process takes place—development of recommendations by the agency to the president of the

United States. It is during this part of the process, which often takes two to three years, that conservationists are making a serious mistake by not following up their recommendations at public hearings with planned input into the development of recommendations by federal agency personnel during the agency review phase of the process. Conservationists must begin to provide citizen input into the decisions being made in this interim period—all kinds of decisions ranging from boundary locations and administrative exceptions, to management criteria and proposed legislation—so that all citizen proposals are considered in their entirety, not just those that confirm the views of agency personnel.

It would be tremendously helpful and educational, not only to the federal agency personnel charged with the responsibility of developing recommendations, but also to the citizen conservationist as well, if once the public hearing is over citizens deeply involve themselves in the decision-making process and stick with a proposal until it reaches the Congress. This can be done by dropping by the offices—local, regional and national—of the federal agencies and meeting those staff members in charge of wilderness review programs. Ask questions such as "How is 'X' wilderness doing?", "Where is it located now in your agency?", "What was your decision regarding boundary adjustments?", "Why did you change this area of conflict and not that one?" and questions of a similar vein. Federal personnel are no different than other people in that they often work in a vacuum with the opportunity to discuss a wilderness proposal only with their peer group—people who think the same way they do. This insulation should not be allowed to continue. Specifically confront them with your views. Try to be helpful and explain why you may disagree with their pending conclusions. They are entitled to the assistance of citizen conservationists and should not be only on the receiving end of verbal or written brickbats. After all, a federal employee is a public servant and, in the absence of dialogue with citizens, it is no wonder that a condescending attitude develops, resulting in introverted, agency-oriented, rather than public-oriented, decisions. So get involved in the wilderness review process—all of it, not just at public hearings —and perhaps you will see decisions more to your liking emerging from the agencies. At the very least, you will be involved in a decision affecting *your* public lands and not be leaving management to the agency alone.

III.
Preserving
De Facto Wilderness

Preserving De Facto Wilderness

By James W. Moorman

De facto wilderness within our national forests is defined by conservationists as areas that are in fact wilderness, but ones not located within any area classified as wilderness or primitive under the 1964 Wilderness Act.

For purposes of the Wilderness Act, there are two types of de facto wilderness. The first type of de facto wilderness is that wilderness found around almost all of our designated primitive areas. This wilderness is subject to review along with the adjacent primitive area. The second type of de facto wilderness is made up of areas that are not adjacent to primitive areas and which, as a result, are not to be reviewed under the Wilderness Act. It is these latter, unreviewable, de facto wilderness areas which I am concerned with here.

There is within our national forests quite a bit of de

Mr. Moorman is director of the Sierra Club Legal Defense Fund. This paper was presented at the Sierra Club's Twelfth Biennial Wilderness Conference, in Washington, D.C., on September 25, 1971.

facto wilderness which should be preserved. Many of you have your own special places about which you know the facts and details. You are probably also aware that cutting is just around the corner under the Forest Service's current search and destroy program designed to convert old growth timber into clear-cuts. You want to take action, but you are afraid your area is going to get lost in the welter of conservation issues now before the public. What can you do?

I am going to suggest what you can and should do. I won't guarantee certain success, but I can say with confidence that you will greatly increase the chances of preserving your area if you follow these suggestions. Furthermore, I believe that if these procedures are followed for all our de facto wilderness areas, then there is a good chance the resulting pressure could change the attitude of the Forest Service with respect to de facto wilderness.

First, a petition, with affidavits, must be filed with the Forest Service requesting that the area of your interest be set aside as a "new study area." The petition should also request a temporary stay of all cutting and other destructive practices until the petition is acted on.

Second, you must get a lawyer and help him in preparing to file two lawsuits: the first should be one to protect the area by injunction in case the Forest Service won't grant your temporary stay. The second should be the eventual appeal from the denial of your original petition.

Third, you must get a bill into both houses of Congress, sponsored by your local congressmen and senators, if possible.

Fourth, mobilize local support to put pressure on the

Forest Service to grant the petition and on your politicians to push your bill through Congress.

Congress has by express provision in the Wilderness Act reserved for itself the exclusive right to create further wilderness areas. Thus, the Forest Service cannot set aside such areas. What it can do, however, is identify areas for congressional approval. Indeed, it is the Forest Service's duty to do so when wilderness classification represents the best use of the area.

In recognition of this obligation, the Forest Service has provided in Section 2321 of the Forest Service Manual that each forest supervisor was to identify not later than June 30, 1972, all areas that are suitable for possible recommendation to Congress as wilderness areas. They are to be designated "new study areas," in the words of the manual.

The function of your petition will be to ensure that your prime areas are included in new study area reviews and to ensure that your forest supervisor does not violate his duty by permitting cutting or allowing roads to be put through areas that should be studied. Getting the service to study an area does not ensure that it will be designated as wilderness, but I believe it greatly increases its chances. "Once begun, half done," as the saying goes.

By a petition, I don't mean a simple request with a few signatures attached. The petition must: (1) Be a statement, in brief form, which tells persuasively why your area should be saved, (2) Be complete, giving all the relevant facts, (3) Be well written so as to *convince*. The press must understand your petition, congressmen and judges must be persuaded by it, and, most difficult of all, the Forest Service must understand it; (4) Be supported fac ly. Attach to your petition the affidavits of people who know the facts: those familiar with the area; who know wilderness and can compare your area to some area already within the Wilderness System; and who know the needs and economics of the local, state and nearby metropolitan populations.

The major points that must be demonstrated by your petition are: (1) that the area is *available* for consideration as wilderness, (2) that it is *suitable* for wilderness designation, (3) that there is a *need* to preserve it as such. It is with regard to this last point that you will need someone who understands economics to help you.

There is an ongoing dispute between the Forest Service and conservationists as to whether availability and need must be shown in the petition before a unit can be designated a new study area. I believe they need not be shown because that is the purpose of the study. The Forest Service, however, says you must demonstrate all three; so to be safe include your arguments on the area's need and availability in your petition.

The officers of the Forest Service will resist, resent, ignore, sabotage, and generally do everything they can think of to thwart your petition. They will not do the one thing citizens should be able to expect from their governmental officials—giving your petition serious consideration on its merits. The Forest Service is so taken by the notion that it has been given the forests to manage as it sees fit that it has forgotten the people may have the right to participate in management decisions. In fact, the Forest Service seems to resent the notion that citizens should have any say, or might inquire about the details of its management.

The chances are almost certain that your petition will

be either ignored or denied by the forest supervisor. Because you cannot expect the Forest Service to act as an evenhanded decision-maker, you must expect a denial of your petition, and you will have to be prepared to follow up your appeal with many subsequent steps. You must make numerous appeals—first to the regional forester, then to the chief of the Forest Service, then to the secretary of agriculture, and ultimately to the courts, starting with the district court. Additionally, you must be prepared for some form of Forest Service action to sabotage your de facto wilderness area, either by permitting timber cutting or by road building, or some other project. Thus, you will have to be prepared to go to court to protect the area while your petition and appeals are pending.

To get a preliminary injunction against the Forest Service requires witnesses and evidence in the form of photos, eyewitness reports, etc. People who have prepared affidavits will come in very handy here. They will be able to make most of your case for you.

In addition to filing petitions and going to court, you should, if it is possible, get a bill before both houses of Congress to establish your area as part of the Wilderness System. Such a bill can have several effects. If Congress does act, the entire wrangle with the Forest Service is short-cut. Also, the Forest Service does respect and fear some congressmen. If you get yours behind you, plus some others important to the service, the service may leave your area alone while your bill is pending in Congress.

As for citizens support: local and state conservation organizations, and local chapters of national organizations, must be rallied to your wilderness area proposal and mobilized for political support. This will have two effects. First, it will help make believers out of your politicians—local, state and national. Second, it will provide you with a good turnout at hearings, once you get the Congress or the Forest Service moving.

The time factor is important. Don't wait until the chain saws are buzzing to go running to your lawyer, your congressmen and your national conservation organizations. By then it will probably be too late. Move first, keep up with events, be prepared, don't be surprised, and don't wait. Every wilderness organization in the country should now mark out what it wants and move ahead with vigor. Otherwise, much cherished wilderness could be lost.

IV.
Action for
Non-Federal Wilderness

Preserving Wilderness Through State Legislation

By M. Rupert Cutler

East of Minnesota and the Mississippi River are located 65 percent of our population but only one-half of 1 percent of our federal wilderness areas. As the 1964 Wilderness Act is implemented and qualifying federal lands are added to the Wilderness System, this ratio will remain constant: even if the 3 million acres of land undergoing review in the East are dedicated as wilderness by Congress, the East's designated wilderness still will constitute only one-half of 1 percent of the envisioned 60-million-acre National Wilderness Preservation System.

For lack of federal land preserved in its natural state, many wilderness enthusiasts, biology teachers and scientists in the East are turning their attention to state-

Mr. Cutler is a doctoral candidate in Michigan State University's Department of Resource Development and a member of Michigan's Advisory Council for Natural Areas. This paper was presented at the Twelfth Biennial Sierra Club Wilderness Conference, in Washington, D.C., on September 25, 1971.

owned land (which, of course, does not come under the purview of the federal Wilderness Act)—land which has more or less been taken for granted in the recent past as we have worked to implement the Wilderness Act.

The twenty-six states east of the Mississippi River administer more than 16 million acres of land in its natural state. Two million acres are within state parks; 4 million acres are fish and game management areas; and more than 10 million acres are in state forests.

Unfortunately, this wealth is unequally distributed, depending on the foresight of each state in years gone by. Twelve of the 16 million acres are located in Florida, Michigan, New York, Pennsylvania and Wisconsin. But other eastern states own more than 200,000 acres of land that deserve tender, loving scrutiny by conservationists. These states are Alabama, Indiana, Maine, Maryland, Massachusetts, New Jersey, North Carolina, Ohio, South Carolina, Tennessee, Virginia and West Virginia. Every state in the East, even Delaware, owns thousands of acres suitable for inclusion in a state wilderness or natural area system.

For clarification purposes, my use of the word wilderness means a tract of undeveloped land, usually of substantial acreage, that appears to have been affected primarily by natural forces other than man. A "natural" area is land retaining its natural character or having unusual flora and fauna, biotic, geologic, scenic or other educational or scientific value, which should be preserved primarily for study and research. A designated natural area may be large or small in acreage and may be part of a designated wilderness area.

In my opinion, every state should have a statute making wilderness and natural area preservation on state-owned lands official policy and providing a legal mechanism under which those lands identified as worthy of special protection by conservationists and scientists can be preserved administratively or by legislation.

Why should dedication of state wilderness and natural areas be made more complicated than other types of administrative zoning now performed routinely on state-owned land? Why not let state agencies simply map out boundaries of areas to be left in an undeveloped condition while the balance is developed for other uses? The preservation of state-owned wilderness and natural areas by all means should be within the context of a comprehensive land use planning and zoning program for an entire state. But administrative discretion in establishing and disestablishing wilderness and natural areas is no adequate substitute for the dedication of areas in perpetuity by state legislatures or bodies with delegated legislative authority.

Our goal, I believe, should be fifty state wilderness and natural area systems based on state laws which complement the 1964 federal Wilderness Act and the administrative research natural area programs now established in federal agencies. Obviously, we are a long way from that goal today.

Several states have created public councils, commissions or divisions to establish systems to protect natural areas. John Humke, now with the Illinois Chapter of The Nature Conservancy, wrote his master's degree thesis in 1970 on "A Comparative Study of Four State Natural Area Systems with Recommendations for Michigan." In it he noted:

. . . . the Michigan Natural Areas Council was found to have a very thorough procedure for selecting and justifying natural areas to be dedicated [by the state Natural Resources Commission]. Wisconsin's Scientific Areas Preservation Board excelled in their methodical approach to establishing a complete scientific areas system. Legislation in Illinois and Indiana gives strong legal protection to dedicated nature preserves. The Illinois Natural Areas Commission is assisting the state in the purchase of over $1 million of privately owned natural areas. In Indiana, a public commission or council was not formed and the natural areas program is being administered by a division of the Department of Natural Resources.

Maryland's new Wildlands Preservation System is based largely on language from the federal Wilderness Act. Prior to establishing this sytem, a "Catalog of Natural Areas in Maryland" was compiled by the state planning department with a federal grant from the Department of Housing and Urban Development. Funds were obtained under the Urban Planning Assistance Program authorized by Section 701 of the 1954 Housing Act, as amended. — Why not seek "701" money for such an inventory in your state?

Other state-level activities have included the 1965 report of the Virginia Outdoor Recreation Study Commission entitled "Virginia's Common Wealth"; Maine's Allagash wilderness waterway legislation of 1966; and the New Jersey Open Space Recreation Plan submitted to Governor Hughes in 1967. Some kind of open space inventory probably has been made in every state in connection with the drafting of state outdoor recreation plans required by the federal Bureau of Outdoor Recreation. Such an inventory may provide a starting point for a more detailed study.

In Michigan, we have considerable potential wilderness and natural areas on state land. Michigan's Department of Natural Resources (DNR) administers 4.5 million acres of state-owned land—.25 million acres in state parks, .5 million acres in game areas, and 3.8 million acres in state forests.

Fortunately, the state has been blessed with farsighted leadership in land preservation. As early as 1926 the Michigan Academy of Sciences proposed "A Suggested Program of State Preserves . . . " In 1949 the state government's Conservation Commission (now the Natural Resources Commission) adopted a policy "supporting the concept of designating natural areas on state land." The Conservation Commission dedicated the first four natural areas on state land in 1951—twenty years ago. In 1952, a committee of the Michigan Botanical Club, which began surveying natural area potentials in the mid-forties, became The Nature Conservancy-affiliated Michigan Natural Areas Council. Since then the state commission has accepted the Natural Areas Council's proposals to dedicate some 100,000 acres as natural areas.

In the last two years, the need for a more systematic approach to the study of potential natural areas on state land and more permanent protection of designated ones became evident. An appropriation to construct a fish ladder for coho salmon on the Presque Isle River, a dedicated "scenic site" within the Porcupine Mountains

State Park, suggested to conservationists that the com-
mission-adopted natural area designation might not provide an adequate degree of protection. Following a successful campaign to kill the fish ladder appropriation,
the Michigan Natural Areas Council prepared legislation
to provide statutory protection for dedicated state-
owned natural areas, in an effort to prevent the Natural
Resources Commission from arbitrarily dedicating a natural area one year, and building a fish ladder or other
nonconforming structure in it the next.

Backtracking for a moment to pick up another thread
of this story, Sierra Club membership in Michigan had
grown by October, 1967, to the point where establishment of the Mackinac Chapter in the state was approved
by the club board of directors. One of the Mackinac
Chapter's explicit goals is a thorough inventory of state-
owned de facto wilderness, followed by whatever action
is required to give these units permanent protection.

Thus, in Michigan early in 1971, we found ourselves
with two groups considering drafting legislation to protect state-owned wilderness and natural areas. The Michigan Natural Areas Council supported a bill to create a
Natural Areas Board, to be appointed by the governor,
which would include the chairman of the Natural Areas
Council. The board would be independent of the Natural Resources Commission, with the power to "determine, supervise and control the management of natural
area reserves" on state-owned, DNR-managed land. In
effect, it called for two equal agencies—the Natural Resources Commission and a new Natural Areas Board—to
administer the same tracts of land.

Meanwhile, the Department of Natural Resources recommended to the governor that he issue an executive

order creating an Advisory Council for Natural Areas which would be advisory to, rather than in charge of, the DNR. The governor signed this order on April 26, 1971. The Advisory Council, composed of six private citizens appointed by the governor plus ex-officio member and DNR Director Ralph MacMullan, meets monthly. It is assisting the DNR in developing criteria and taking inventory of existing and potential natural areas.

Unknown to either the Mackinac Chapter of the Sierra Club or the Natural Areas Council, Donald L. Law, a University of Michigan Law School senior and member of the Environmental Law Society at Ann Arbor, had chosen to write a state "Wilderness Act of 1971" as his term project in a spring 1971 course in legislative drafting. Using the federal Wilderness Act as a starting point, with input from environmental law professor Joseph L. Sax, Don Law drafted a bill which later was transformed from class exercise to real legislation when it was introduced on April 27, 1971, in the Michigan House of Representatives as House Bill No. 4881 by Ann Arbor Representative Raymond Smit. The bill was cosponsored by a bipartisan group of House members.

To say that the people who had been pondering wilderness and natural area legislation were surprised when they heard of H.B. 4881 would be an understatement.

Conveniently, Don Law became staff counsel to the House Conservation Committee and helped schedule early hearings on the bill. At a June 9 House hearing, massive support for the principle embodied in H.B. 4881 was evident from organized labor, sportsmen, backpackers and botanists. Even the oil and gas industry applauded the concept of state land use zoning, for clarification of where it can and cannot operate.

After more than two months of negotiation, a compromise bill, "House Bill No. 4881, Substitute 2," finally emerged to the satisfaction of almost everyone concerned. The perfected piece of legislation combines some of the features of both Don Law's and the Natural Areas Council's original bills. In summary, this "Wilderness and Natural Areas Act of 1971" does the following:

(1) It defines three kinds of areas to be established on state-owned land: (a) wilderness areas—3,000 acres or larger, or islands of any size; (b) wild areas—less than 3,000 acres, but with "outstanding opportunities for personal exploration, challenge or contact with natural features of the landscape"; and (c) natural areas—of any size, with features of special educational or scientific value.

(2) It provides for the creation of a Wilderness and Natural Area Advisory Board within the DNR—essentially, statutory recognition of the governor-appointed Advisory Council for Natural Areas—to "make recommendations for the dedication and administration" of these areas.

(3) It gives the DNR six months to make an initial inventory of its lands, to find all areas suitable for inclusion in the three categories and to propose such dedications to the Natural Resources Commission. It must conduct a similar review annually. Citizens may also propose the dedication of such areas to the commission.

(4) It stipulates that all such proposals, whether made by the DNR, the Advisory Board or private citizens, must be acted upon within ninety days.

(5) It provides that hearings, with advance notice, must be held by the commission before any wilderness, wild or natural area can be designated or declassified.

(6) It rules out alteration in the land except for that

needed to provide minimal appropriate access, to preserve or restore plant or wildlife species, or to document scientific values. Also prohibited are granting of easements, condemnation of dedicated lands, exploration for and extraction of minerals, commercial enterprises, utilities and permanent roads.

We consciously steered away from giving our state legislature the role carved out for Congress under the federal Wilderness Act—that of approving all wilderness area designations—for two reasons. First, our Natural Resources Commission has a good record of protecting undeveloped areas in the state; second, we see less difficulty winning endorsement of protective designations by the commission (whose rule-making authority is a form of delegated legislative power) than by the legislature.

In short, we now have a bill supported by conservation groups and by the DNR—one which industry apparently thinks it can live with. [The bill passed the Michigan House of Representatives on November 5, 1971, by a vote of 90 to 3.] We face the challenge of convincing a less enthusiastic Senate committee of its merits.

On the whole, the future of wilderness on state-owned land in Michigan is bright. It remains only for a coalition of conservation organizations to dedicate itself to this project until the goal is accomplished. Although much hard work lies ahead, we are optimistic.

Preserving Wilderness Through State Legislation- As a Legislator Sees It

By Francis W. Hatch, Jr.

As a Massachusetts legislator, I have had some problems with my topic, "Preserving Wilderness through State Legislation." It is not that I am against enacting state laws to preserve and to require sensible use of wilderness. It is just that in my state, as in most urban states in the country, vast tracts of remote, undeveloped land which would qualify as the kind of wilderness one sees in some of our national parks simply don't exist. In Massachusetts there is only one exception, Monomoy Island, off Chatham on Cape Cod, which was declared a wilderness area by Congress in 1970. A special commission is now studying open space in Massachusetts and all of New England to inventory landscape features and natural areas that should be preserved. I regret to say that the odds are overwhelmingly against finding even one new wilderness in Massachusetts.

Mr. Hatch, a Massachusetts state representative since 1962, authored the Massachusetts Wetlands Act. This paper was presented at the Twelfth Biennial Sierra Club Wilderness Conference, in Washington, D.C., on September 25, 1971.

Assuming I'm wrong, however, and that this commission produces one or two serendipities which would qualify as card-carrying Sierra Club wilderness areas, I don't think we'd get the result we want.

The nub of the question, it seems to me, is that even if we in state government exert superhuman effort, and vote to appropriate fortunes, we will end up acquiring only a relative handful of wilderness areas in a few states. Rather, the opportunity for comprehensive preservation lies in peripheral, less dramatic areas: in wetlands, in smaller parcels of undeveloped land, in property publicly and privately held by conservation commissions, municipalities, charitable groups and even individuals.

Therefore, I shall use sections "A" and "C" of the *American Heritage Dictionary*'s definition of the word "wilderness": "any unsettled, uncultivated region left in its natural condition especially, A. a large tract of land covered with dense vegetation or forest," and "C. a piece of land set aside to grow wild." It seems to me that these definitions, particularly "C," accurately reflect the wilderness that we in urban states are destined to know. (Because of our paucity of wilderness, I have carefully omitted mention of a third definition of wilderness, "B. an extensive area that is barren or empty such as a desert or ocean or waste.")

Consider Massachusetts. We now have approximately 400,000 acres of land set aside for conservation purposes—the bulk of it in forests, parks and water districts under state or municipal management. Other governmental property owners include 296 conservation commissions throughout the state. One hundred twenty of these commissions have already spent $3.5 million of their communities' tax dollars, matched by an equivalent state appropriation, to acquire 11,000 acres of undeveloped land. None of these acres could qualify as wilderness; nevertheless, adjacent to centers of population, they are welcome pockets of open space which would not have existed if our legislature had not had the foresight to create the nation's first community conservation commissions in 1955.

Success of the program is reflected by our state expenditures in matching funds, which swelled from $6,650 in 1962 to more than $600,000 in 1970. Even this figure does not accurately reflect the real extent of the interest in preserving undeveloped land, because in 1970 alone municipalities requested more than $2 million in matching funds for land acquisition.

In the private sector, conservation land trusts are beginning to blossom. To some individuals, it is much more attractive to give land to a private trust than to sell or donate it to a community conservation commission. Acreage set aside in these trusts does not yet approximate that held by the conservation commissions, but frequently directorates overlap, which allows for coordinated planning and acquisition.

Further evidence of concern by our private citizens is the successful campaign to preserve a 250-acre peninsula in Boston Harbor, known as Worlds End. In 1969 $449,000 was raised in only twelve months by the Trustees of Reservations to purchase the site.

In Massachusetts, the most effective method of preserving large tracts of quasi-wilderness would be through our fresh-water and salt-water wetlands acts. As all of us are well aware, these swampy, mosquito-infested backlands were never of much interest until the population explosion pressured developers to find marginal, cheaper tracts of land to develop.

In 1965, I sponsored a stopgap bill to permit the state to review plans for dredging or filling fresh-water wetlands so that critically important ones would remain untouched until the state had an opportunity to restrict their use. The reasoning behind the measure was that while municipalities felt that swamp development was a matter of only local concern, in fact it oftentimes has regional ramifications. Therefore local communities should not make the final decision on whether to dredge or fill.

In 1968, we enacted a more comprehensive measure to restrict development of these wetlands in perpetuity. The stakes are big. According to surveys, there are 300,000 acres of inland wetlands, in parcels of ten acres or more, which must be protected.

We have also enacted similar legislation to protect the state's 50,000 acres of salt-water wetlands. To date, 18,500 acres have been officially restricted, while hearings have been held to set aside an additional 25,500 acres.

These four acts—two inland and two salt-water wetland measures—eventually will result in a unique method of preserving open space and of creating a number of mini-wilderness areas in perpetuity. Although the procedures are unfortunately cumbersome and time consuming, the program in its entirety will nearly double the amount of restricted open space from the present 400,000 acres to 750,000.

Similar approaches have been taken in other New England states. Vermont has a law restricting development of all lands higher than 2,500 feet, which is based on much the same principles as Massachusetts' wetland protection laws; the Maine legislature, filling a void left by municipal inaction, has effectively zoned the entire state, while Rhode Island has a new coastal zoning law. These laws, and other measures that I will mention later, are all examples of the exercise of a state's police power —regulation without compensation—which can protect the maximum acreage for the least amount of money.

So much for some of our New England regulatory statutes which affect and create potential wilderness. What day-to-day steps can a state legislator like yours truly take to maintain the wilderness that still exists?

Sometimes a lawmaker's most constructive action is not to act; not to approve measures that nibble away at the dwindling supply of parkland unless adequate replacement acreage is available; not to permit indiscriminate development of portions of state forests, even by interested factions within state government, and so forth. And, of course, oftentimes after good environmental legislation is enacted, persistent and insidious attempts are made to cripple its effectiveness. Legislators must always keep their eyes and ears open, particularly during the waning days of a session when crippling bills or amendments to programs are frequently offered.

There are also a number of more positive steps we can take. We now have three pieces of proposed legislation being debated in Massachusetts, and three more which have just been signed into law.

One, a scenic rivers bill, would make development of designated river basins exceedingly difficult. Here again, the problem is that in an industrial state like Massachusetts most of the rivers aren't as scenic as they used to be, even a decade ago.

A second measure would enable the state Department

of Natural Resources to create a statewide system of scenic trails, which would complement a 1969 act permanently protecting the Appalachian Trail where it passes through Massachusetts.

A third bill, modeled after federal legislation, would require agencies of the state government to file impact studies on every proposed project that would disturb the environment. Highway construction projects are obvious targets because all too often these affect wetlands, lakes and even the more subtle aspects such as a community's sightliness.

A fourth proposal authorizes a $5-million bond issue to enable the state to buy wetlands. [On October 6, 1971, this proposal was signed into law, Ch. 839, Massachusetts Acts of 1971.] This is the first time we have voted state funds to purchase wetlands. The greatly increased cost of ownership, as opposed to restricting use of wetlands, naturally limits the number of acres that can be set aside, but purchasing power is an extremely valuable lever to have available as a last resort. The Hockomock Swamp, 6,000 acres of virtual wilderness thirty miles south of Boston, is a good case in point. Much of this wetland should be acquired by the state now because only imposing restrictions on its use could result in another case of doing too little too late.

In August, 1971, Massachusetts Governor Francis Sargent signed into law legislation giving ten taxpayers the right to proceed in court against polluters. In 1969 I filed the first comprehensive bill in Massachusetts on the citizen's right to action. It was based almost entirely on the Michigan statute, and, of course, has been altered substantially as opposition mounted. It is now a much weaker measure, which allows only lawsuits based on enforcing existing state regulations, but at least it is law. Once we amend it to allow the citizen to proceed against municipalities and the state government, we will have a much more satisfactory piece of legislation.

Two major projects in my area of the country are of national significance. One of these is the acquisition by the state Department of Natural Resources of thirty Boston Harbor islands so that their use and development can be properly planned. In 1970 $3.5 million was voted by the legislature for this purpose. The other project is the Connecticut River National Recreation Area proposal in the western part of the state.

So much for pending legislation. There is one vital, unresolved problem that must be considered. It involves the crucial question of privately owned, undeveloped land. How should this land be taxed? If an individual is going to be assessed at the top value based on residential acreage, it will be virtually impossible for anyone except the very rich to hold open land. In the end, even the rich will be forced to relinquish these holdings to developers.

Nowhere is this being more clearly demonstrated than in the small coastal town of Castine, Maine, at the mouth of the Penobscot River, where I am an all-too sporadic summer visitor. Recently, the state of Maine passed an excellent statute which includes protection for both its coastline and rivers. This landmark statute prohibits development of riverbank and shorefront property unless adequate zoning exists in the municipality. The town was recently revalued, using as a yardstick the selling price of acre-lots on a scenic point with a picture-book view of the Camden Hills. Even though this was mercifully the first (and I hope the last) experience the town has had with an aggressive outside developer, the consequences have been disastrous for many people. The ensuing valuation of $125 per shorefront foot will clearly make it difficult for Mainers to retain their shorefront property, some of which has been in families for generations.

Clearly this is a dilemma which must be resolved, because it is unrealistic to expect government and private charitable agencies to be able to set aside enough undeveloped land to meet demands for wilderness and recreation needs. Individuals must not be unduly penalized for trying to help. But they are, because most present town tax and county zoning laws encourage and, indeed, are based on financially beneficial use of land, rather than uses that fit long-range community needs. For example, in 1966 I bought a large abandoned farm in Vermont. For years hunters have prowled the mountainside it sits on. I feel they should be allowed to continue to do so. With the shortage of acreage for sportsmen, to say nothing of open land for pure recreation, it seems to me essential that we landowners err on the side of public use rather than public posting. Yet, if I, a nonspeculator, am ultimately going to be taxed on the basis of what the land would bring as housing lots, it will be difficult to keep from selling it off, bit by bit, just to stay even.

We must find a means of shedding the crushing burden of the real estate tax. National attention is being focused on the recent California court decision that disallows real estate tax revenues for school purposes. The ultimate impact of this decision is not on education but on the environment, where it could have enormously beneficial consequences. As real estate taxes spiral,

property owners are driven to consider increasingly un-
desirable uses of their land. If, however, income or some
other source of taxation ultimately supplants real estate
as the cornerstone of a community's tax base, the pressure of taxation on open land could be relieved greatly.

We must also find ways of making more imaginative
use of our open space by encouraging organizations that
own tracts of land to adopt sensible and compatible use
of it. You cannot blame a financially strapped school
committee for casting a covetous eye on twenty unused
suburban acres, clogged with brambles and beer cans,
for which the tax-exempt, charitable owner has not provided a land use plan.

We in state legislatures, perhaps by passing enabling
legislation, can encourage communities to overhaul their
present restrictive zoning and subdivision laws. Planned
unit development would work wonders for our precious
supply of remaining open space.

I am certain that this and other problems critical to
the environment will be answered and answered soon,
not just by Massachusetts but by all state governments
singly and together, when appropriate, through regional
solutions. The fact of the matter is that there is too
much pressure and too much awareness of the dire consequences for legislation not to be passed.

The final problem I raise is a very real one which I
think should be of concern to everyone in government
and particularly to members of interested environmental
organizations, such as the Sierra Club. Assume for the
moment that every single arrow that is needed has been
supplied for our quiver to protect the environment—
wetland bills, environmental impact studies, citizens'
right to action, the whole gamut. This is a realistic ex-

pectation—by 1976, not just in Massachusetts but throughout the country—thanks·to the efforts of conservation groups.

We will then be faced with the most critical task of all: how to make the statutes work. Make no mistake, lack of citizen concern creates a vacuum; and in a vacuum, any level of government does what it likes to do most—defers making the hard, unpopular decisions necessary to get a program moving and to keep it on target. Unless there is enormous pressure from constituents, these statutes and regulations will wither. I have seen this firsthand in Massachusetts. Enforcement of my own wetlands act has been very uneven to say the least, and under the 1968 inland wetlands act, use of only a few acres of swamp has been restricted. Granted, there are difficulties; there always are in any new venture. But I am convinced that if we cease and desist after state laws are fashioned to our liking, our victory will have been pyrrhic indeed. Wilderness, whether in Monomoy Island or suburban form, must not only be protected, but, indeed, it can be created provided we act now.

Legislators truly talk a good environmental game when we vote for programs, but we often fail to back up this initial commitment when it comes time to vote funds for enforcement personnel or technical assistance. It seems to me that the business of creating and protecting wilderness requires lasting involvement and dedication from three essential parts of state government: legislators, members of the executive branch, and the personnel within the various state agencies. I like to picture these groups as a three-legged stool—which will perform its designated function only if the members of the Sierra Club, and other concerned citizens, sit on it.

Wilderness and Natural Areas in the Southeast

By Keith A. Argow

Wilderness and natural areas in the southeastern United States are those that fall south of the Grit Line—the line south of which one is served grits for breakfast, like them or not.

The number of areas in the Southeast that might qualify for preservation under the Wilderness Act is small compared to that in the West. Nevertheless, there are many tracts of land that clearly merit preserving in their wild, natural state. And there are other ways of saving them. One alternate strategy for preserving relatively small tracts of wild land is to designate them as "Natural Areas," primarily for scientific research and study.

Dr. Argow is administrator of the Mount Rogers National Recreation Area, Virginia, for the U.S. Forest Service. He is also the Appalachian representative of The Nature Conservancy and a member of the board of directors of the American Forestry Association. This paper was presented at the Twelfth Biennial Sierra Club Wilderness Conference, in Washington, D.C., on September 25, 1971.

Natural Areas

According to the Society of American Foresters, "a natural area is a tract worthy of being preserved to exemplify typical or unique vegetation and its associated biotic, edaphic, geologic and aquatic features in as near natural condition as possible, primarily for purposes of science and education." Generally, tracts designated as natural areas are relatively small, having a primary value for ecological study.

In the Southeast there are natural area programs operated by a number of federal and state agencies, educational institutions and several private organizations. The Natural Area Council in New York, the Audubon Society and The Nature Conservancy have made major contributions to this latter effort, as has the southern forest industry whereby five corporations have reserved natural areas. Most industry programs have emphasized setting aside small tracts of land with unique residual stands of old-growth timber because of their research value and historical interest. Among those companies participating in the Southeast are International Paper, Union-Camp, Westvaco and Duke Power Company. In Tennessee, the Bowaters Southern Paper Corporation has reserved four scenic tracts, such as waterfalls, as "pocket wilderness" and has constructed access trails to these areas.

Unlike wilderness areas, which are clearly defined by federal legislation, the definitions and criteria for natural areas vary according to the administering agency, state, corporation, university or private organization that owns and manages each unit.

Much technical guidance for establishing natural areas has been contributed over the years by the Society of

American Foresters (SAF), the nation's organization of professional foresters. The SAF has encouraged "reservation of an adequate number of natural areas representing examples of all significant forest and forest-related vegetation in the country. The society cooperates with other professional, scientific and private groups—local, state, national and international—to assure the creation and maintenance of such a system. Normally, the SAF does not own land; instead, it works through the affiliation of its members with public and private agencies who have jurisdiction over forest land." The SAF Natural Areas Program is the largest organized effort to seek out, register and protect small native sites in the United States.

In the Appalachian Section of the society (comprising Virginia and the two Carolinas) a permanent committee of twenty-three volunteer foresters geographically distributed throughout the three states looks after these areas and periodically proposes additional tracts. It has been my privilege to be chairman of this program for the past eight years, and more recently, to have a seat on the national Natural Areas Committee of the SAF. In the Appalachian Section, there are thirty-five registered natural areas—twenty in North Carolina, eight in South Carolina and seven in Virginia. A directory with maps and descriptions of each tract will be published by the Society of American Foresters in 1972.

Research Natural Areas

Reserved tracts administered by the several federal land management agencies are referred to as "research natural areas." In 1968, the Public Land Law Review Commission estimated that these scattered areas com-

prised 900,000 acres of public land in the United States.
They are not administered under a statute such as the
Wilderness Act. Instead, they are coordinated by an ad
hoc committee composed of representatives of their federal agencies. The committee has no budget, but it is
working toward establishing uniform management for
these federal lands and compiling detailed data on all
such natural areas in the country, including those owned
by states and private interests.

Set aside mainly for research and educational purposes, research natural areas are generally not intended
for recreational pursuits, which could harm the natural
community of flora and fauna. The Research Natural
Areas Program of the Forest Service is the oldest of the
federal agencies' programs. Twelve of its eighty-eight
units are located in the Southeast and encompass 3,120
acres. Similar programs are operated throughout the
Southeast by the Fish and Wildlife Service (27,320 acres
in eighteen areas) and the National Park Service (320
acres in one area). Other federal agencies with such programs include the Atomic Energy Commission (10 acres
in one area) and the Tennessee Valley Authority (275
acres in two areas).

Natural Landmarks

In addition to its research natural areas, the National
Park Service conducts the Natural Landmarks Program:
a register of geological and biological wonders in many
ownerships located throughout the nation. Surveys are
continually underway to identify new natural landmarks; one hundred seventy sites have already been designated. When land is registered as a natural landmark,
the owner (usually private) receives a certificate and a
plaque and agrees not to modify the land to an extent

that would diminish its natural landmark qualities. The government does not acquire the land or rights to use it, and the owner may sell at any time. If a new owner alters the land, the natural landmark designation may be revoked.

The new National Environmental Policy Act requires that due consideration be given to natural landmarks in the evaluation of federally funded programs. Thus, by appropriate identification and recognition, the natural landmarks program offers at least minimal protection to natural areas.

State Programs

Several southeastern states have large state parks which they manage under environmental policies similar to those of the National Park System. These lands, acquired primarily for recreation, comprise a variety of wild areas. Four southern states have established natural area programs within their state park systems. Georgia has created an independent agency, the Georgia Natural Areas Council, to administer its program. In 1971, the Alabama legislature considered a bill to establish a similar agency. Tennessee has enacted legislation entitled The Natural Areas Preservation Act of 1971 which provides for "the recognition of natural areas having outstanding scenic, biological, geological and recreational values." Many southeastern universities, particularly those with programs in forestry and land management, have acquired such lands and reserved them as natural areas.

Citizen Programs

In recent years private organizations such as The Nature Conservancy have had notable success in preserving wilderness and natural areas in the Southeast. This 26,000-member organization, now in its twenty-first year, is the only national organization solely devoted to the preservation of environmentally significant land. Nationwide, it has been instrumental in protecting 210,000 acres of wild lands.

One of the Conservancy's projects in 1970 was to preserve more than 11,000 acres of high ground, oceanfront and marsh on Virginia's Atlantic coast. In the first of two major acquisitions, the organization purchased the 8,750-acre Smith Island group made up of Smith, Ship Shoal and Myrtle islands for $1.25 million. The islands were named for Captain John Smith, who landed there in 1608. Owners have included families of George Washington and Robert E. Lee. Until the Nature Conservancy intervened, the Smith Islands were destined to become the site of an intensive-use resort development which would have destroyed their fragile salt marsh ecology. A second acquisition of Virginia barrier islands involved the purchase of 2,475 acres of the 3,600-acre Hog Island, important for its wetlands and use as a major rookery. The Hog Island purchase includes control of the adjoining 7,500 acres of salt marsh.

Sixty-five miles southwest of Miami, the Conservancy is involved in the preservation of Lignumvitae Key, which has retained the natural complex environment destroyed elsewhere in the Keys. The Conservancy is purchasing Lignumvitae and nearby Shell Key to be set aside as a natural area under the protection of the state of Florida.

In South Carolina, the Conservancy and the National Audubon Society are raising $1.5 million in a joint effort to preserve 3,400 acres of Four Hole Swamp, one of the finest cypress stands remaining. This tract, 4½ miles long and 1½ miles wide, contains trees up to five feet in diameter, and is a haven for a variety of wildlife.

Although such spectaculars attract public attention, about one-half of the Conservancy's projects last year were little publicized, and involved lands donated by their owners. These lands are usually turned over to an appropriate unit of government or similar organization with a reverter clause stipulating development restrictions of use. Occasionally cooperative agreements are used. By this method, ninety preserves are now available for study by thirty-one colleges and universities around the country, most of these in the heavily populated East.

One important function of The Nature Conservancy is to purchase private inholdings on public lands and hold them until such time as funds are appropriated for federal and state agencies to acquire the land. A recent example was the purchase of a critically important tract within the St. John's National Wildlife Refuge in Florida—a habitat for the endangered dusky seaside sparrow. A similar project involves an attempt to acquire land for the Appalachian Scenic Trail in advance of developers, who have other objectives in mind.

Land and Water Conservation Fund

Among the surest ways to secure wilderness and natural areas for posterity is outright acquisition of the land. Forest-based industries, while cooperative in protecting small tracts with scientific value, cannot be expected to support programs that deny availability of the raw wood materials they depend upon.

In the South, unlike the Northeast, Midwest and West

Coast, state bond issues for open space and park land acquisition have been uncommon. Most public acquisition in the region in recent years has been financed largely with the states' share of the Land and Water Conservation Fund, plus the program of federal agencies in national forests, parks and wildlife refuges.

The fund was established by Congress in 1964 and is financed by the sale of federal real estate, offshore oil lease revenues, and recreation entrance fees (Golden Eagle Passports). Sixty percent of the dollars appropriated by Congress for the fund go to the states on a matching basis. The remaining 40 percent is allocated to the federal land management agencies. Although both the state and federal apportionments from the Land and Water Conservation Fund have been used to acquire key wilderness inholdings in the Southeast, the fund's greatest benefit has probably been in the acquisition and development of intensive-use recreation areas, thereby relieving some pressure on designated wilderness and natural areas that already show signs of overuse or incompatible use.

A good example is the 46,000-acre tract recently optioned by the U.S. Forest Service in Virginia within the Jefferson National Forest. Located close to the population centers of the East, and with an interstate highway running through it, this acquisition will provide many opportunities for hunting, hiking and more intensive recreational development for camping. Parts of the area are also being studied for possible inclusion in the Wilderness System.

Wilderness Areas

None of the foregoing review of related programs is

meant to imply that priceless tracts of full-fledged wilderness do not exist in the Southeast. In fact they do, and some of the most extensive tracts lie within the Great Smoky Mountains National Park. Under review procedures set by the 1964 Wilderness Act, hearings have been completed on potential wilderness areas within the park, but no formal proposal has been made by the National Park Service.

In Virginia, hearings have been held on Shenandoah National Park, and a proposal for a 73,000-acre wilderness area was introduced in Congress in 1971. If approved, it will constitute the first formal wilderness in the Old Dominion.

The oldest federal wilderness areas in the Southeast are administered by the U.S. Forest Service. These include the Shining Rock and Linville Gorge areas in the Pisgah National Forest in North Carolina.

The National Wildlife Refuge System also offers opportunities for wilderness preservation in the Southeast. Reviews have recently been completed on the following refuges: St. Mark's in Florida, Cape Romain in South Carolina, Okefenokee Swamp in Georgia, and Cedar Keys in Florida. Congressional legislation was introduced in 1971 formally to establish wilderness areas in Okefenokee and Cedar Keys of 345,000 and 378,000 acres, respectively.

There are extensive tracts of private lands (which do not fall under the purview of the Wilderness Act) which merit consideration for some sort of protection. One of those in the news today is Baldhead Island, which includes 12,000 acres of remote maritime forest and marsh, at Cape Fear on the North Carolina coast. Currently, it is being developed as a resort area by the Carolina Cape Fear Corporation, although the Conservation Council of North Carolina is working to raise funds to secure the island in its wild state.

The 1971 summer issue of The Wilderness Society's publication *The Living Wilderness* magazine listed all wilderness proposals introduced in Congress during 1971. In fact, The Wilderness Society keeps an up-to-date record of all pending wilderness proposals, for those who wish further information.

In addition to the areas mentioned, there are several citizen proposals for wilderness classification: the 12,000-acre Sipsey de facto wilderness in the William Bankhead National Forest, Alabama; and the Cranberry, Dolly Sods and Otter Creek de facto wilderness areas (totaling 65,000 acres) in the Monongahela National Forest, West Virginia.

Although the issues and crises in wilderness and natural area preservation persist, the time left to resolve them diminishes. Public and private efforts to secure these lands must quicken, for once destroyed the values cannot be easily recovered. Our expanding population and its increasing appetite for second homes, material goods, new roads and reservoirs are exacting a final toll from the remaining wild lands in the Southeast. These places are important for their uniqueness and proximity to large population areas. Far-sighted planning and action to secure these lands should continue and even be stepped up. We must try harder. There is still time for decision, but it is running out.

V.
Action for
River Wilderness

Status of the Wild and Scenic Rivers System

By Jules V. Tileston

To most people, the words "wilderness" and "wild" create a vision of a spacious area of mountains, forest, or desert where one is alone with nature. A challenge is implied. But there is another resource offering solitude and a ready chance to savor nature—free-flowing rivers.

The concept that rivers merit protection in their free-flowing condition is not new. As early as 1905 at least one state, Wisconsin, had recognized that free-flowing rivers were important public resources. This was reaffirmed in 1937 when the state refused to permit construction of a hydroelectric project which would have flooded a portion of the Brule. But it was not until the early 1960s, when national attention focused on the struggle to pass the Wilderness Act, that much thought was given to the need for a national policy to preserve

Mr. Tileston is assistant chief of the Division of Resource Area Studies, Bureau of Outdoor Recreation, U.S. Department of the Interior. This paper was presented at the Twelfth Biennial Sierra Club Wilderness Conference, in Washington, D.C., on September 25, 1971.

and protect our best remaining free-flowing rivers for the benefit and enjoyment of present and future generations.

One of the first tasks in preparing protective river legislation was to inventory the resource potential. In 1963 the secretaries of agriculture and the interior compiled a list of 650 rivers, or sections thereof, which had special qualities. With primary emphasis upon geography and type of river, sixty-seven were selected for initial screening by interagency field teams. I was the leader of one of these teams. As a result of reconnaissance inspections of all sixty-seven rivers, criteria and a study approach were developed. These techniques were then used to conduct in-depth studies of twenty-two river areas appearing best to represent the type of river deserving national recognition. The studies were the basis for drafting, and later supporting, the legislation known today as the Wild and Scenic Rivers Act. Like the Wilderness Act, the Wild and Scenic Rivers Act is a product of much individual and group effort by members of Congress, conservationists, state groups and federal agencies.

Early we learned that there was much confusion over the meaning of the term "wild" river. "Wild" was selected because it was a catch phrase; but we also wanted to protect rivers that were not wild in the wilderness sense. Today, after almost eight years, we still find major misconceptions about the term. The legislative history of the act sets down several simple but fundamental points. The task of preserving and administering free-flowing rivers is not one that can or should be undertaken only by the federal government. Different streams need to be preserved and protected for different reasons—some solely for their values as completely natural streams, and others for recreational opportunities. It is recognized that these objectives are not always compatible. The area protected need not be large. In many instances, the desired public control should be possible without fee acquisition.

Following passage of the act in 1968, the Departments of the Interior and Agriculture, as the two principal administrators, set up machinery to coordinate the program. An interagency steering committee was formed to interpret and implement it. The Bureau of Outdoor Recreation has the staff role on this committee and also is responsible for administering the provisions of the Land and Water Conservation Fund, which provides funds to the states to plan, acquire and develop wild, scenic and recreational river areas included in state outdoor recreation plans.

On October 2, 1968, when the Wild and Scenic Rivers Act became law, eight rivers with a combined length of 392 miles became part of the National Wild and Scenic Rivers System. These included portions of the Clearwater, with its tributaries, the Lochsa and Selway rivers, Idaho; Eleven Point, Missouri; Middle Fork of the Feather, California; Rio Grande, New Mexico; Rogue, Oregon; Upper St. Croix-Namekagon, Wisconsin and Minnesota; Middle Fork of the Salmon, Idaho; and Wolf, Wisconsin. These eight rivers had three things in common: they were noncontroversial, they had very strong support for preservation, and much of their riverbanks was already in public ownership. Many other rivers were given varying degrees of consideration for inclusion, but for one reason or another were dropped.

A second group of twenty-seven rivers having a total

length of 4,650 miles was listed as potential additions to the system. These had two things in common—some controversy, and strong support for preservation. Each river is to be studied, and reports outlining its qualifications to be submitted to the president and Congress by October, 1978. Each report must include an evaluation of what would be gained, lost, or curtailed if the river were added to the national system; a recommended administrative agency (federal, state, local, or some combination of these); and costs to the federal government. In the East are located the Penobscot, Maine; Delaware, New York and Pennsylvania; Pine Creek, Clarion, and Allegheny, Pennsylvania; Youghiogheny, Maryland and Pennsylvania; Little Beaver and Little Miami, Ohio; Maumee, Ohio and Indiana; Pere Marquette, Michigan; Lower St. Croix, Wisconsin and Minnesota; Upper Iowa, Iowa; Gasconade, Missouri; Buffalo and Obed, Tennessee; Chattooga, North Carolina, South Carolina, and Georgia; and the Suwannee, Georgia and Florida.

Although either the Bureau of Outdoor Recreation or the National Forest Service has chief responsibility, studies are conducted on an interagency basis with the full and active help of state and local governments. The act requires that the final report be reviewed by the governor of the affected state, the chairman of the Federal Power Commission, the chief of the Army Corps of Engineers and other concerned federal agencies, and that their comments be incorporated in the final recommendations before they are sent to the president and Congress.

A look at the types of rivers specifically listed in the Wild and Scenic Rivers Act gives an idea of what the system might ultimately be like. There are true wilderness rivers like the Middle Fork of the Salmon, upper portions of the Selway, the Rio Grande, and the Oke-fenokee Swamp portion of the Suwannee. Rivers like the Upper Iowa and Gasconade flow through land pri-marily devoted to agriculture. Rivers with operating power dams over eighty feet high form reservoirs up to ten miles in length. The river flows in some cases such as the Youghiogheny are directly regulated by dams. In at least one instance, there is rather substantial develop-ment in the river and along the shore: the section of the Allegheny listed in the study group flows through down-town Pittsburgh.

Units of the system are managed and developed ac-cording to criteria established in the act. There are three classes of rivers: (1) wild, (2) scenic, and (3) recreation-al. A river may be in more than one class, as long as a meaningful recreation experience is possible. Overall values are very important, but prominent factors are the degree and type of access; the extent and type of devel-opment along the shoreline and the watershed; and water quality.

The special values of a river in the national system are protected in two ways—by control of land use within a narrow corridor along the river's edge, and by control of water resource projects. Control of land use is designed primarily to assure that incompatible uses do not take place, and that there is no substantial interference with proper public use and enjoyment of the river and its immediate environment. The act restricts the boundaries to an average of not more than 320 acres per mile, or a one-quarter-mile strip on each side of the river, and limits fee acquisition to not more than an average of 100 acres per mile. State and local governments are encouraged to adopt and implement compatible land use plans for areas under their jurisdiction. Mining is permitted in all but wild river areas, subject to rules and regulations to provide safeguards against pollution and unnecessary impairment of the scenery. In designated wild river areas, minerals are withdrawn from all forms of appropriation under the U.S. mining and mineral leasing laws.

With regard to water resource projects, the act prohibits the Federal Power Commission's issuing a license to construct facilities on or directly affecting a river included in the system. Other federal water project plans and programs must be reviewed in advance by the secretary of the interior, or if national forest lands are involved, by the secretary of agriculture. Prohibited projects are those determined by the appropriate secretary to have a direct and adverse effect; and invade the protected areas or unreasonably diminish the scenic, recreational, and fish and wildlife values present when the river was added to the national system. The act also provides similar restrictions on permits issued by the Corps of Engineers and other forms of cooperative federal-state programs such as those sponsored by the Soil Conservation Service. Reports and recommendations submitted to Congress for authorization of funds for a federal water resource project affecting a protected river area must indicate clearly how the proposal would affect the river's special environment. Similar protection for up to eight years is also afforded to the twenty-seven rivers specifically listed in the act for study as potential additions to the national system.

In addition to those rivers already within the system, and those on the study list, a third group of rivers is recognized. The secretaries of agriculture and the interior are authorized to conduct studies to determine which additional free-flowing river areas in the nation deserve special consideration whenever a federal planning program is started. Identification under this procedure—the so-called 5(d) list—requires the planning agency to include in its final report an evaluation of free-flowing characteristics in a degree comparable to the report's other aspects, such as irrigation or flood control. Identification is based upon sufficient investigation determining that substantial free-flowing values exist, but it does not mean that the river qualifies for inclusion in the National Wild and Scenic Rivers System. There has been considerable confusion over this aspect because some people have assumed that such a river is protected and that a wild and scenic river study is scheduled. These assumptions are incorrect. The only protection afforded is equal treatment to the free-flowing values of the river in the final report—something which has not been given in the past. Detailed wild and scenic river studies are initiated only when another federal agency, such as the Corps, Bureau of Reclamation, or the Federal Power Commission, starts a planning program. Forty-seven rivers now have this status.

The Wild and Scenic Rivers Act provides two means for adding rivers to the national system: an act of Congress (whenever direct federal administration is involved), and approval by the secretary of the interior (when protective action and administration is at the state level).

The first method, an act of Congress, normally would be preceded by a study and recommendation to Congress by either the Department of the Interior or Agriculture. This has been the procedure for the twenty-seven rivers on the list of potential additions. The report and recommendation could arise, also, as a result of studies done for other purposes. Three such examples are: the studies on the Big South Fork of the Cumberland in Kentucky and Tennessee done by Agriculture, Army, and Interior under a provision of the 1968 Flood Control Act; the Rappahannock-Salem Church Project in Virginia, as part of a postauthorization study by the Corps in combination with a so-called 5(d) identification; and the proceedings before the Federal Power Commission on the proposed High Mountain Sheep Dam and related hydroelectric generating proposals on the Hells Canyon portion of the Snake River in Idaho and Oregon.

The second method, approval by the secretary of the interior, requires an act of the state legislature and the request of the governor. The secretary evaluates the request to make sure the river area meets the criteria established in the Wild and Scenic Rivers Act and the supplemental guidelines adopted by the departments of Agriculture and the Interior in February, 1970. Such a river area must be wholly and permanently administered in a manner consistent with the special values of that river area without cost to the federal government. Administration, therefore, must be at the state or local level. If these conditions are met, the river is then added to the National Wild and Scenic Rivers System and accorded all the protection and stature of federally managed rivers in the system. In many ways, this procedure is analogous to putting the best state parks in the National Park System while not modifying state administrative responsibilities.

The Wild and Scenic Rivers Act listed two candidates for inclusion pursuant to state action—the Wolf River in Wisconsin, and the Allagash Wilderness Waterway in Maine. In July, 1970, the secretary of the interior, at the request of the governor of Maine, approved the Allagash as the first state-managed unit and ninth component of the National Wild and Scenic Rivers System.

As for preservation systems on the state level, in 1963, only one state had an official system of free-flowing streams. There are now eighteen state systems. Fourteen states are considering legislation to develop systems, and four are investigating the feasibility of establishing their own programs. Three other states have identified rivers which, in their opinion, merit potential inclusion in some future stream preservation system. Altogether, states have identified more than 600 streams and rivers in a free-flowing condition having substantial values.

How are reviews proceeding under the Wild and Scenic Rivers Act? Studies for most of the twenty-seven rivers specifically required by the act are now underway. The first few have taken longer than anticipated—primarily because we are working under a new program. We are hopeful, nevertheless, that what we have learned will enable us to speed up the process. The Suwannee and Upper Iowa are undergoing final review. The Clarion and Chattooga have been sent to the state governors for official review. Studies on the Delaware, Lower St. Croix, Little Miami, Allegheny, Youghiogheny, Pere Marquette, Buffalo (Tennessee) and Obed are well underway and should be completed within the next year.

Where do conservationists and groups such as the Sierra Club fit into the Wild and Scenic Rivers Program?

They are the eyes and ears necessary to make sure nothing happens unalterably to commit the resources of free-flowing streams until all the pertinent facts have been considered. Within this context, they must be active, alert, and informed. When appearing in support of or opposition to a proposal, they should know the area as well, if not better, than anyone else; know the people involved and their concerns; know the facts related to the proposal and its alternatives; and be prepared to take a positive position on what they will support. Emotion is fine and has its place, but it is no substitute for a logical, reasoned presentation.

Personally, I would like to see more nongovernmental studies and reports on free-flowing river areas. The 1970 report prepared by the Northern California Conservation Committee of the Sierra Club on the Tuolumne River is a concise document clearly setting out the conflicts and relevant values needed to make a decision for the best use of Tuolumne. I might add that this report was largely responsible for the inclusion in 1970 of the Tuolumne on the 5(d) list.

A final thought—conservationists should not wait until everything is all "planned." To be most effective, they need to be in on the planning from the start. This is not easy, and most of all requires persistence.

Battling for River
Preservation in Tennessee

By Liane B. Russell

Few states are blessed with such a variety of truly beautiful rivers as is Tennessee. Few states have the distinction of providing running water which tempts not one but two of the major dam-building agencies of this country. Tennessee has yet another, happier, distinction: it was the first state to establish a comprehensive state scenic rivers system. The federal Wild and Scenic Rivers Act, which became law six months later, covers two Tennessee rivers; a third river deleted at the last minute was made the subject of a special federal study.

Three stories of partial success illustrate clearly the various types of initial threats conservationists should be familiar with in any river campaign, the methods by which various levels of safety have been achieved in Tennessee, and the new problems that arise at these levels.

Dr. Russell is a geneticist and helped to found the Tennessee Citizens for Wilderness Planning in 1966. This paper was presented at the Twelfth Biennial Sierra Club Wilderness Conference, in Washington, D.C., on September 25, 1971.

Our Tennessee river variety includes the tumbling streams emerging from the highest mountains in the eastern United States, the deeply cut sandstone gorge rivers of the Cumberlands, the watercourses flanked by limestone bluffs and arching trees that characterize the Highland Rim and Central Basin, and, finally, the meandering cypress swamp rivers of west Tennessee. There were many more of all of these not so long ago. But two agencies have vied with each other for years to still the flowing waters. The Tennessee Valley Authority (TVA) has authority over the extensive watershed of the Tennessee River, while the Army Corps of Engineers controls the Cumberland River drainage. The TVA often boasts that the shoreline of its reservoirs measures more than 10,000 miles, greater than the combined shoreline of all the Great Lakes.

My first story concerns the group of rivers protected by our state Scenic Rivers Act. A fuller account of the passage and content of this act has been published.[1] I shall analyze briefly the reasons behind our success in getting the act passed, the reasons why it was weakened in passage and thereafter, the problems in its implementation, and its overall effects. Throughout this story, my use of the word "we" indicates a number of highly able, dedicated volunteers of the Tennessee Citizens for Wilderness Planning and the Tennessee Scenic Rivers Association.

Some of the factors that led to success in the state scenic rivers effort are common to all conservation campaigns: a handful of people who cared more about what

[1] *Sierra Club Bulletin*, Vol. 4, No. 1, January, 1969.

they were working for than about losing sleep or leisure or pay, thorough research of the facts, and a concerted effort to disseminate our story to the news media, legislators and other organizations. We managed to write a good bill based partly on federal scenic river legislation which was then pending, and partly on thorough knowledge of rivers in Tennessee. Our legislative sponsor was energetic, knew his way around the Tennessee General Assembly, and was, at least to start with, popular there. We were fortunate in that one of us could keep a close watch "on the hill" in Nashville, which afforded quick reaction to sudden dangers or opportunities. And, finally, we were dealing with a legislature in which there was, in the beginning, no organized opposition and which was, in fact, willing to remain ignorant of the content of most bills, judging them mainly by their sponsors.

Almost by accident, opposition was stirred up by a small group of local politicians who were hoping to get a dam on the Obed. At the hearing that was called on the bill, they made quite an emotional show about "outsiders trying to lock up *our* river." It is not clear whether the dam-promoting agencies worked behind the scenes to defeat or weaken the bill. Perhaps it is significant that TVA, which months before had determined that the Obed dam could not be justified (the benefit-cost ratio being only 0.6:1.0), delayed publication of this finding until after the hearing and house vote—at which a legislator from the Obed region removed from the bill not only the Obed and its tributaries but, for good measure, the other river system in his district, the Big South Fork of the Cumberland. Other rural politicians, alarmed by the cry of "outsiders" at the hearings, followed suit and about half the rivers were removed.

One other interesting source of opposition which emerged during the subsequent campaign in the state senate turned out to be a U.S. congressman, who tried to influence a state senator to remove a river because of pork-barrel considerations on the federal level.

Despite these deletions, a very good basic bill passed the legislature, designating eight rivers and one creek for immediate inclusion in the state Scenic Rivers System. The bill is a lengthy and thorough document of about twenty sections. Its main features may be briefly summarized as follows. (1) It contains fine quotable language on the intent of the state to preserve rivers. (2) It includes rivers for immediate designation and provides for the process of adding rivers. (3) It establishes three classes of rivers according to certain characteristics. Associated with these classes land uses of various levels of restrictiveness, and land areas of different width, are permitted. (4) It provides for upgrading of a river or segment into a higher class, and forbids management that would lead to downgrading. (5) It provides for acquisition in fee title, or preferably of scenic easements, *and* allows the exercise of eminent domain.

Unfortunately, a convention of local legislative courtesy exists, which allows removal of a river if the local legislator so much as mentions it. In 1969, one year after passage of the scenic rivers bill, the Buffalo River was removed by special amendment. But by the same mechanism two rivers have since been added. For this reason, it is very important to make friends for a state scenic rivers system in the regions where the rivers are located—not just in the urban centers where most of the organized conservationist support is found. It is difficult to do this because rural populations often look upon outsiders with suspicion, especially if they have come to advocate government interference. By the same token it is an easy matter for enemies of river preservation to exploit this situation.

The case of the removal of the Buffalo from the Tennessee Scenic Rivers System serves as a good illustration. Real estate promoters from outside the area were reported to have agitated the local farmers into a frenzy of unfounded fears. The farmers were convinced that inclusion of their river in the system would mean they would be fenced off from it, their cattle could not go down to drink from it, they would be charged six dollars per day to use it, and hippies would camp along the banks, lighting fires which might threaten their woods. The truth of the situation—that the farmers would actually be paid (in the form of scenic easements) for the opportunity of continuing their present land use practices—could not be made to penetrate. The farmers arrived in Nashville in force and sat shouting in the gallery until the Buffalo fell before their onslaught. One fault of our law is that it does not set up any impediments to removal of rivers from the system.

Probably the most effective way to convince local citizens of the benefits of including their river in the state system would be to show them how well it works for other rivers. Unfortunately, 3½ years after passage of the act, the state was still to acquire a single scenic easement, although it now appears to be on the verge of doing so. Acquisition funds are available, but our Conservation Department is strapped for salaries; the staff assigned to this program consists of one part-time person. The vigorous public education program which could do wonders to allay false fears has gone by the wayside. Sometimes, an aroused uninformed landowner can cause direct damage, as in a recent negotiation when one declared to the state official, "All right, you shall have your scenic easements, but it sure won't be very scenic when you get it," whereupon he got out his chain saw and cut every one of the huge hardwoods along one mile of riverbank. Hopefully, this case is not a typical one.

Despite not yet being implemented, the state Scenic Rivers System has already done some tangible good. Its existence was a big factor in squelching at least one TVA proposal for a dam. And in certain state government agencies there is a growing awareness of the system which has served to color the state's dealings with federal agencies.

My other two stories concern two specific rivers—the Obed and the Big South Fork. Both were on the original draft of our state bill; both were removed because of pending dam proposals which whetted the appetites of local power structures. One of the rivers is in TVA territory; the other is controlled by the Corps. The major justification for the dam proposals were flood control for the Obed and hydroelectric power for the Big South Fork. In both cases supposed recreational benefits from the resulting reservoirs were thrown in as a strong second justification.

It was the threat to dam the Obed which triggered my own and my husband's personal involvement in active conservation work, and was one of the major factors leading to the formation of the Tennessee Citizens for Wilderness Planning. It also led to our first encounter with TVA and a peculiar creature of TVA's Tributary Area Development Program, a "Watershed Development

Association." Such groups of local citizens are theoretically created to study the resources and needs of the area and then, in cooperation with TVA, to develop a plan for improvement. In practice they are often dam-promoting groups which provide the grass-roots support for new projects. This was certainly true in the case of the Obed. While a few members of the local power structure sat on the board of the Watershed Development Association and talked loudly about preventing recurrence of the 1929 flood at Harriman (a freak occurrence, incidentally) the bulk of the local population did not know the facts, did not know the river (which is rather inaccessible, in a deep gorge) and did not really care. A nearby farmer was shocked to find out from us that the planned reservoir would put his house and some of his fields under fifty feet of water.

Our first task was to advertise the beauty of this unknown river and to dig out facts to counter the claims being made to justify the dam. We found real ammunition in an almost forgotten 1939 TVA study. TVA itself had stated, in essence, that only about 200 acres were at risk in the city of Harriman, that these could be protected by flood-plain zoning (which had since been done), and that it was easier and cheaper to move existing structures out of the flood plain than to build a dam. It became obvious to us that the new TVA study would have to add a huge recreational benefit—undoubtedly phony in an area already saturated with reservoirs—to make the benefit-cost ratio exceed 1.0. We spread that word as much as possible. At the same time, we tried to acquaint key people with the beauty of the Obed. The congressman of the district was floated down it; editors of two major newspapers were enticed there. Illustrated talks were given to dozens of civic clubs. We even managed to get the head of the TVA Recreation Department and a visiting consultant to go there for a swim and picnic.

The successful arousal of public sentiment and unearthing of critical facts eventually led TVA to publish its findings indicating that the dam was not economically justifiable. As I stated above, this news was released too late to help keep the Obed in the state scenic rivers bill.

In the meantime, we were working to get the Obed and two other rivers included in national wild and scenic river legislation. Even while the battle in the state legislature was taking place, we were testifying at hearings in Washington. We elicited supporting testimony from the Tennessee Game and Fish Commission and Department of Conservation, Senator Albert Gore, two of our nine congressmen, and a considerable number of Tennessee organizations. We used a sort of snowball approach. Each time we managed to elicit support from one source, we distributed this news to other hoped-for sources of support, saying in effect, "Won't you, too, join us?" I believe one thing that helped at congressional hearings in Washington, D.C., was that we had prepared an estimate of the cost of acquiring scenic easements for the three rivers we proposed for inclusion in the national rivers system, and were able to supply this estimate when asked about it by congressmen. So the Obed and its tributaries were included in the study category of the National Wild and Scenic Rivers Act, together with the Buffalo. We lost our third river, the Big South Fork, because of the peculiar circumstances under which the bill finally passed, which I shall not relate here.

Because of the work load on the underbudgeted Bureau of Outdoor Recreation's regional office, the Obed study has suffered one delay after another. It was slated to be completed by fall, 1972. In the meantime, a series of threats to the wild status of the river have developed; these have had to be fought from the early stages. TVA planned a major powerline to cross the Obed and a tributary. Although TVA would not move the line, it finally agreed to build the towers far back from the rim and hang the wires by helicopter to avoid disturbing the vegetation in the valley. A strip mine was opened for a one-mile stretch of the gorge. Public pressure caused TVA to cancel the contract and to embark on a model reclamation job. Other strip-mine permits in the watershed have been applied for; the state has had to be encouraged to deny such permits until the BOR study is completed. A real estate development is being built at the only major road-crossing on the river—and the developer is using some of our own laudatory remarks about the river in his advertising copy. Fighting these threats requires on-the-spot vigilance and constant contact with state and federal agencies, although some things, like the real estate development, cannot be stopped until the government acquires control over use of the land.

My third river story is about the Big South Fork of the Cumberland, which lies in the Army Corps of Engineers' territory rather than TVA's. The Big South Fork is a major sandstone gorge river, with many intimate and enchanting tributaries. As I stated above, the river had been deleted from the state bill and was later lost from the national bill, thanks to the peculiar legislative vicissitudes associated with that bill's passage. The proposed dam was the 483-foot high, $200-million Devils Jumps dam, "justified" on the basis of hydroelectric power and recreation. Because of our efforts against Devils Jumps, the erstwhile congressional sponsors of the dam, Senators Cooper of Kentucky and Gore of Tennessee, inserted a paragraph into the 1968 Rivers and Harbors Bill ordering two new studies. One of these was a restudy of the proposed dam, to be done by the Corps, and the other was an interagency study of alternative plans for "recreational, conservation, or preservation uses."

We resolved to have as much input as possible in this latter study. By contact on all levels with the agencies directly or indirectly involved, as well as with some of our congressional friends, we managed to change the direction of the study in a number of ways, e.g., by enlarging the study area. We supplied a great deal of factual information on flora and fauna, ecology, geology, archeology, history and float characteristics, and we mapped a proposed national park boundary. After familiarizing ourselves with the area, we offered guide services to members of the study team and organized hikes and floats for them, supplying canoes and other equipment. The interagency study of alternatives that emerged is acceptable. Devils Jumps and two other possible dam sites are rejected in all but one of the six major alternatives.

In the meantime, the Corps' own restudy of Devils Jumps dam is almost two years overdue. We dare to hope that this is because the Corps realizes too many people have been made aware of the scenic resources of the river and the economically unjustifiable nature of the dam. Most people, including Tennessee's current senators, believe the proposal is dead. The Corps' failure to file its restudy report, however, has delayed consideration of the officially proposed alternatives. As in the case of the Obed, delay has had adverse effects. Oil was struck in the area, although the boom may now have passed its peak. Uncontrolled strip mining on one major tributary has filled the once-clear river with silt. Sportsmen's groups have come out against the national park proposal because it would bar hunting. And so on. It is clear that a temporary waning of the dam's threat is not enough, and that some positive protection must be legislated soon. We favor a national park, possibly with an adjacent national recreation area. A national recreation area by itself would not give enough protection to this very fragile area. We shall need much help from our friends in Kentucky, where political support must be mobilized for this interstate proposal. We have been promised that protective legislation will be introduced, although present indications are that far too small an area will be included and far too little protection spelled out. Obviously, the type of effort that will be required of us now will be different from that needed to fight the dam. Nevertheless the mobilization of public support will again play a big part.

Following is a summary of prerequisites for other conservationists, drawn from some common denominators of our experience, which may be typical of river preservation battles in the United States.

(1) The complete, unswerving dedication of at least one person who in turn can mobilize others. There should be freedom to act quickly, without cumbersome board meetings, etc.

(2) Research, to acquaint yourself thoroughly with all pertinent facts. Mobilize as many experts as you can.

Get to know your area thoroughly through field trips and map study. Be sure you are factually correct before you make statements. Expertise makes you unassailable, convinces others to support you, and impresses politicians.

(3) Contacts, constantly and at all levels (especially the personal one) with staffs of pertinent agencies, related or rival agencies, legislators and their staffs, and representatives of the news media. There are "good guys" in all agencies, and many are anxious to help when they realize your intentions are unselfish, and your opinions based on a wealth of information.

(4) Attempts at all stages to inform others, to get them interested and involved. Talk and write about your cause at all possible opportunities. Use visual aids; get members of the news media, politicians and just plain people personally acquainted with your campaign. Get other organizations to support you and make it easy for them to do so by drawing up a resolution with an endorsement form they can simply sign. At all stages use the snowball effect; anytime you get support, bring it to the attention of potential supporters.

All the points above apply to rear-guard actions in specific instances when rivers are under attack. I feel we must also work to put an end to the attacks themselves. We should give strong endorsement to a proposal for a bill of rights stating that our rivers are to be left free-flowing and natural unless Congress specifically rules in given instances that national economic benefits "will clearly outweigh environmental losses" and that there is no feasible alternative to change.[2] The burden of proof must be on the despoilers.

Until we have such a bill of rights, we must promote

[2] Miller, James Nathan, *Reader's Digest*, July, 1971.

legislation to establish an independent body (other than the promoting agencies) to determine the environmental impact of river projects and to calculate their benefit-cost ratios. Such an independent body could be made up of a rotating membership of experts of university caliber. Public hearings should be mandatory early in the course of these evaluations. There should be no way in which funds could be appropriated for a project until the independent evaluation clearly showed they should be.

We must support a public education program to teach that rivers are not local property to be used or despoiled for supposed local or personal benefits, but living things which only pass by the local scene, and belong to all who wish them well.

The Fight to
Save the Oklawaha

By Marjorie H. Carr

Since the days of sailing ships and pirates, there has been talk of digging a canal across Florida. No serious consideration was given the idea until the thirties when, during the Depression, a sea-level canal was approved as a work-relief measure. The work was begun in 1935, but the project was abandoned in 1936, partly because of threats to the water supply and partly because shippers did not really seem interested in using a cross-Florida canal. Nevertheless, since there was money to be made merely by digging canals and building locks and dams, the canal proposal was modified, reworked and restudied. Finally, with fanfare that included puffs of red, white and blue smoke provided by the Army Corps of Engineers, the Cross-Florida Barge Canal was begun again in 1964.

Mrs. Carr helped organize the Florida Defenders of the Environment and is active in conservation campaigns in that state. This paper was presented at the Twelfth Biennial Sierra Club Wilderness Conference, in Washington, D.C., on September 25, 1971.

Seven years later, after $50 million had been spent, and the project was nearly one-third completed, a U.S. district court judge granted a group of conservationists a preliminary injunction against further canal construction. Three days later, President Nixon issued a statement halting the entire project, saying, in part:

I am today ordering a halt to further construction of the Cross-Florida Barge Canal to prevent potentially serious environmental damages.

A natural treasure is involved in this case of the Florida Barge Canal. It is the Oklawaha River—a uniquely beautiful, semitropical stream, one of a very few of its kind in the United States. The Oklawaha would have been destroyed by construction of the Canal.

The step I have taken today will prevent a past mistake from causing permanent damage. But more important, we must insure that in the future we take not only full but also timely account of the environmental impact of such projects—so that instead of merely halting the damage, we prevent it.

Behind these two dramatic events there lies a story of citizen action sustained through nearly ten years.

In the fall of 1962 our local Audubon society (the Alachua Audubon Society of Gainesville, Florida) sponsored a series of evening programs on current environmental problems in Florida. Although at that time we had no idea that the Cross-Florida Barge Canal (CFBC) project would pose serious environmental threats, we did know that it would inevitably bring about changes. Accordingly, we invited two gentlemen representing state and federal agencies to report on the probable effects of the project on the Florida environment. The talks they gave were straightforward accounts of canal construction plans and the economic benefits of this massive federal project. They reassured us of the Corps of Engineers' concern for the sanctity of the Floridan aquifer, and of its admiration for the beauty and integrity of the Oklawaha River.

The talks were well prepared and illustrated with slides and charts. They obviously had been presented many times before. Canal proponents had every reason to expect their presentation would generate good public relations. Gainesville, however, is a university town, and many of our Audubon members are professors who have a habit of questioning and testing statements. A blizzard of questions followed the presentation—questions about the economics of the project, and about the effects of construction on the geology, hydrology and ecology of the canal project area. These were questions for which the government speakers had no satisfactory answers. The audience that had come to the meeting with a completely neutral attitude toward the canal project went away that evening disturbed, uneasy and determined to find out more about the probable effects of the CFBC on the Florida environment.

In January, 1970, a citizens' group called the Florida Defenders of the Environment (FDE) published a report entitled "Environmental Impact of the Cross-Florida Barge Canal with Special Emphasis on the Oklawaha Regional Ecosystem." This 118-page report was written by twenty-six scientists, economists and land planners. The authors were assisted in the preparation and publication of the report by some seventy-three concerned citizens—mostly scientists. All the work was done on a volunteer basis by men and women willing to take action in defense of the environment. In a way, this report was made possible only because some curious conservationists decided to find answers to worrisome questions raised at an Audubon society meeting in Gainesville, eight years earlier.

It did not occur to any of us, as we went home that evening, that we were starting out on a campaign which would in time enlist the active support of the leading conservation organizations and of thousands of individuals throughout the nation; which would be supported by donations amounting to $80,000, collected from contributions averaging $10 per person; which would be publicized by articles in national magazines, newspapers and by network television programs; and which would mobilize the scientific community of Florida. A new type of conservation organization was formed—the Florida Defenders of the Environment—comprising a coalition of more than 300 scientists, economists, lawyers, land planners and citizens who have used their special skills and knowledge in preparing documented reports on specific environmental problems throughout the state.

Today, Florida Defenders of the Environment, Inc., is a nonprofit organization dedicated to the protection of environmental quality in Florida through the preparation of special reports based on reliable information. FDE reports are made available to the public and may serve as the basis for environmental policy and decisions, or necessary legal action. FDE consists of a board of trustees; an executive board made up of four officers and the chairmen of the scientific, legal, economic and land-planning advisory committees; a small permanent staff, and its membership. Policy is determined by twenty-nine trustees representing different sections of the state and areas of specialization. Officers, committee chairmen and staff are responsible for FDE activities. Members of the advisory committees evaluate the merits of projects being considered. Membership in FDE is open to citizens who will use their special skills and knowledge in defense of the environment. With the exception of a full-time executive coordinator and part-time secretarial help, all FDE work, whether scientific or general office assistance, is volunteer. Most of the daily office work—answering correspondence, keeping our extensive files up to date, telephoning—is handled by a corps of volunteers who spend at least one day each week working for FDE.

Florida Defenders work closely with other conservation groups in the state. Indeed, the close cooperation of the several strong conservation organizations in Florida has resulted in a statewide force which is flexible and respected, and has the clout of immense citizen support. Ten years ago it was quite a different story, here in Florida.

It did not occur to us back in 1962 that we had grabbed a tiger by the tail. We just wanted to find some answers. We just wanted to know the true state of affairs. We wanted some facts. But that is the key to success in any conservation effort. Get the facts—and then act. Get all possible information pertaining to all the different facets of the problem, making sure to differentiate between facts and someone's opinion or interpretation of those facts. Once you have surveyed the assembled information—dependable information—your most effective course of action is usually quite obvious. If you get the facts, the press will tell your story, government agencies will take action, legal suits can be documented, and the president may even intervene on your behalf.

This dependence on accurate information will require a filing system and good record-keeping, no matter how short and simple the effort may turn out to be. In our FDE files in Gainesville we now have more than 2,500 items concerning the CFBC project, exclusive of a mountain of correspondence and newspaper clippings. Our system is simple. Each incoming item is given a sequential file copy number, marked in red ink. Corresponding file cards are made for a master index catalog for both author and subject. Articles of special interest are cross-indexed. Although this may seem like a piddling housekeeping detail, in any volunteer effort it is important to set up a system that makes it convenient for an ever-changing group of people both to assemble information and to extract it.

The main consideration in keeping files of pertinent information is, of course, the needs of your group. But good files have an added advantage. Other groups— writers, governmental agency representatives, university students—will use them for research on the project in question. I can think of at least a half dozen well-known writers who have spent two or three days each carefully going over material in our files. The resulting articles were enormously helpful in furthering our campaign.

In assembling the facts needed for any effort, begin at the beginning. First, get straight exactly what is going to happen, and where and when it will happen. Government agencies draw up detailed work plans. These plans are public property and you have a legal right to look at them. In many cases the agency will provide you a copy, and at the very least it will permit you to make your own. We found the Army Corps of Engineers, for example, to be very cooperative in this respect. We have copies of all its many project reports and addendum reports on the CFBC project, and also a complete series of its detailed maps.

Next, it is essential that you assemble all the available material describing the geophysical, biological and geographical characteristics of the area. Maps and bulletins prepared by the U.S. Geological Survey, supplemented by any state geological publications and by soil maps prepared by the U.S. Department of Agriculture, will usually give a pretty good description of the physiographic features of the terrain involved. It will probably be more difficult to find published material covering the biological features. But biologists are wide-ranging creatures, and even if you are unable to locate published accounts of the ecology of your area, you can be pretty sure that a large number of biologists, with assorted interests, have done field work in the region. This is the way it was with the Oklawaha, and when it came time to publish our environmental impact report, several biologists contributed to the series of short descriptions of the various sections of the threatened area.

The next step is to stop and assess the probable effects of the proposed project on the environment. This assessment is often a matter of mere common sense, but it is good to get experts to review your conclusions. For example, during the early years of our effort several anticanal people suggested that the cross-state canal would sever the Floridan aquifer and cause south Florida to become a desert. If true, this would have been a devastating accusation. Inspection of the Corps' construction plans, however, indicated that the channel of the barge canal would, for the most part, penetrate only the surface of the lime-rock. Consultation with geologists revealed that while they had reservations about the effect of the canal project on water quality, they certainly could not support the idea that it would affect the supply of water in south Florida. At that time, proper hydrologic studies for the area were lacking. Today, the Corps would not be permitted to start digging a canal until the project's impact on the water regimen of the area was thoroughly described. Still, consultation with experts is helpful when trying to reach accurate assessments of probable effects.

It should be noted that when the canal project was revived in the late fifties, many responsible individuals and organizations, such as the Florida Federation of Garden Clubs and the Florida Audubon Society, seriously questioned the Corps as to the effect—the impact—of the canal construction on the Oklawaha River. This is the answer they received (and what, in essence, we were told at our memorable meeting in the fall of 1962). I quote part of a letter written in 1965 by our U.S. congressman:

Your concern about possible effects of construction of the Cross Florida Barge Canal on the beautiful and priceless Oklawaha River is certainly understood. However, fears of its destruction may well be dismissed in the light of information I have obtained from the Corps of Engineers.

I am informed that only part of the Oklawaha between Sharpes Ferry and the proposed Rodman

Dam near Kenwood will be altered by the canal construction. The lower seven miles of meandering channels which interlace its delta as it flows eastward into St. Johns, will remain undisturbed. From Sharpes Ferry to Moss Bluff and then upstream the river will not be changed by the construction of the dam and the canal. Furthermore the canal will follow along reasonably straight lines which will leave many of the old meanders of the river in their natural state. The project will also provide large stable pools that are expected to be quite attractive for visitors, including fishermen. A number of bays will be formed along the boundary of Ocala National Forest which will surely enhance that part of the forest. The Corps recognizes . . . possibilities of maintaining the natural conditions and plans for their consideration wherever practicable.

Although some changes will necessarily be made to accommodate the barge canal, there will apparently be many of the Oklawaha River values retained.

That sounds pretty reassuring, doesn't it? Only that part between Sharpes Ferry and Kenwood to be altered. But do you know where Sharpes Ferry and Kenwood are? You are probably as well informed about the location of these places as we were. It was not until we had carefully examined good maps and the Corps' project plans for the river valley that we realized what actually was going to happen. Although the Oklawaha is about eighty miles long, it is really the lower forty-five miles—the part below the point at which the river receives the massive flow from Silver Springs—that has brought the river its fame as one of the sixty-three outstanding wild rivers of the nation.

In these lower reaches the Oklawaha has carved out a mile-wide valley which supports a dense hardwood swamp-forest. What the Corps planned to do was to build two dams across this valley and to dig the canal channel straight down its middle. Thus, a thirty-five-mile-long stretch of the river and its forested valley would be flooded, and the remaining ten miles of river would have its flow drastically reduced.

So the impact of the CFBC on the Oklawaha would be effectively to destroy it. Here was a major threat to the environment and one we were sure could be avoided. Having found that action was needed, and what that action should be, we then had to learn precisely who had the authority to effect a change in the project plans. We learned that the Army Corps of Engineers answers only to Congress and the president. Congress controls the Corps through appropriations of money, and the president is its commander-in-chief.

I believe it is very important for conservationists to find out who has the power to modify a plan that threatens the environment. Time and money are too scarce to be spent haring off after someone who cannot do anything to correct the problem. This is not to say you should not ask help from other influential people. Ask for just that—for their help in persuading the authorities to take action. During our long campaign to save the Oklawaha we kept a large number of people informed about what we were doing. Periodically, we would brief the Florida delegation to the U.S. Congress, the governor and members of the state cabinet, the heads of state and federal agencies, chairmen of key congressional committees, and, of course, the heads of all conservation organizations. In most cases the response would be merely an acknowledgment, but occasionally somebody would come through with a very helpful suggestion. And we always felt that in an emergency we could ask any of these people for advice without having to introduce ourselves and explain our problem. They all were well aware of what we were trying to do.

In seeking help, whether it be from a politician, from a professional, from conservationists, from a bureaucrat or from your best friend, you ought to keep in mind that a given conservation effort appeals more to one person than to another. Anyone leading a specific project ought to recognize and be prepared to take advantage of this fact. Moreover, he should not be downcast when someone from whom help has been expected fails to come through.

It is also essential to communicate with your supporting public. Do not hesitate to ask people to write letters or donate money, or both. Be frank, brief and specific in your request, and always quickly acknowledge a donation with a thank-you note. FDE now has the names and addresses of more than 3,000 people who have written letters or donated money in support of the fight for the Oklawaha. Many of these people have been on our rolls as Friends of the Oklawaha for more than eight years, and have responded to appeals for help over and over again.

We should have saved the Oklawaha by 1966. By that time we had made the impending destruction of the river known to all concerned government agencies, to elected officials, and to the growing body of people who were concerned over the wasting of the land. By that time it was well known that, at best, the economic justification of the canal project was highly dubious. But we did not win then. Politicians, including the president, apparently had not correctly assessed the volume of public concern over the environment. In Congress the old pork-barrel politics continued—they still do today—and the Corps kept receiving appropriations for canal construction in the Oklawaha valley. We realized then that our only recourse would be the courts. But we were unable to find lawyers interested in environmental problems of this kind.

So we just waited. We did not give up; we waited. And that points up one more exhortation to conservation activists. Do not give up until your objective is irrevocably lost. You will find that many of your supporters, after repeated disappointments, will suggest that you call it quits and turn your attention to some other problem. This attitude is to be discouraged. In fact, I think it might be helpful if, during the early stages of a given effort, the leaders define for themselves exactly what their objectives are, and then, by some solemn oath or other, pledge to work until they have either won or truly lost. In our case, it was fairly simple. We wanted to save the Oklawaha. The river was still flowing in its wooded valley. We would not quit until it was destroyed.

For the next two years a dozen or so of us did little more than telephone each other now and then to reassure ourselves that we had not quit but were only waiting.

Then one day *Sports Illustrated* published an article about the Environmental Defense Fund. One of our group read the article and telephoned that organization. EDF task force lawyers came down, and within two months the whole Save-the-Oklawaha, anticanal fight was on again, stronger than before. This time we turned out so fast that our opponents seriously believed we had been given $5 million by the railroads.

Well, you are familiar with the rest of the story. The fight for the Oklawaha is nearly over. At the moment we are having some trouble getting the water drained out of the Rodman Reservoir. Canal interests are obstructing the move but the problem will probably soon be resolved.

Meanwhile, we are working to insure that a wise land use plan for the Oklawaha regional ecosystem is developed. Some forty outstanding Florida architects and land planners—all volunteers—have already prepared a preliminary plan.

It will take twenty years for the damaged part of the Oklawaha to heal itself. But long before that this superb stream will be recognized as one of the great wild and scenic rivers of our nation.

VI.
A World Heritage Trust

A World Heritage Trust

By Russell E. Train

The United States is exercising strong and continuing leadership in international environmental affairs. A prominent example of our interest in this field is the World Heritage Trust—an exciting concept put forward by President Nixon in February, 1971, whereby areas of great natural and cultural value around the world may be preserved for the benefit of generations to come. First, the background and context to this proposal.

No place is immune to the major environmental impacts which our technology is producing. We are slowly coming to learn that we all belong to one, closely interrelated world system. And it is essential that we work together to protect and preserve that system, for we have no other.

In transmitting to Congress his recent message entitled "A Foreign Policy for the Seventies," President

Mr. Train is chairman of the Council on Environmental Quality. This paper was presented at the Banquet of the Twelfth Biennial Sierra Club Wilderness Conference, in Washington, D.C., on September 25, 1971.

Nixon stated: "We know that we must act as one world in restoring the world's environment, before pollution of the seas and skies overwhelms every nation."

One of the most heartening developments of our time is that the nations of the world are finally coming to recognize this blunt fact, and are beginning to cooperate in various ways to protect our common natural heritage.

Recently, this government has engaged in a series of cooperative environmental activities with other nations. Canada and the United States have cooperative agreements for joint action on mutual environmental problems such as pollution of the Great Lakes. In October, 1970, at the request of the president, I visited Japan and met with Prime Minister Sato to initiate regular collaboration between our two countries on environmental matters, which was continued by the visit of a Cabinet-level Japanese delegation here in June, 1971. Again at the initiative of President Nixon, the North Atlantic Treaty Organization has established a Committee on the Challenges of Modern Society, to which I am the U.S. representative. This committee has achieved important agreements in a variety of areas of environmental concern, including oil spills. Within the Organization for Economic Cooperation and Development, the major developed countries are working together on environmental matters, with particular emphasis on the trade and other economic aspects of environmental problems, and the Economic Commission for Europe is providing an important forum for exchange of environmental information between East and West.

Finally, it is our hope that the June 1972 conference in Stockholm on the problems of the human environment will have developed a framework for effective international action for environmental protection.

"Stewards of the land"—how often we have heard that phrase used to define man's responsibility to protect the land he has inherited.

Rafting down the incomparable Colorado with my family in summer, 1970, was a unique personal experience which would have been impossible but for the dedicated stewardship of many conservationists.

To walk through the bush of the Serengeti Plains in Tanzania, surrounded by the herds of grazing wildebeest and zebra, is to step back into time, into the springtime of the earth—another incomparable experience only made possible because a few men and women cared enough and acted in time.

These areas and others like them have a significance which transcends merely local interests. In a very real sense, they belong to all of us. Certainly, when such an area is destroyed or damaged, all the world is poorer for the loss.

It is the recognition of this fact which has given rise to the idea of the World Heritage Trust and which led our government to make an international agreement establishing such a trust a major objective.

While such a concept has been urged in the past—notably by the IUCN—President Nixon's February 1971 Message to Congress on Environment was the first time that this dramatic idea was put forward as an official policy by any government. The following are the words of the president:

As the United States approaches the centennial celebration in 1972 of the establishment of Yellowstone National Park, it would be appropriate to mark this historic event by a new international initiative in the general field of parks. Yellowstone is the first National Park to have been created in the modern world, and the National Park concept has represented a major contribution to world culture. Similar systems have now been established throughout the world. The United Nations lists over 1,200 parks in ninety-three nations.

The national park concept is based upon the recognition that certain areas of natural, historical, or cultural significance have such unique and outstanding characteristics that they must be treated as belonging to the nation as a whole, as part of the nation's heritage.

It would be fitting by 1972 for the nations of the world to agree to the principle that there are certain areas of such unique worldwide value that they should be treated as part of the heritage of all mankind and accorded special recognition as part of a World Heritage Trust. Such an arrangement would impose no limitations on the sovereignty of those nations which choose to participate, but would extend special international recognition to the areas which qualify and would make available technical and other assistance where appropriate to assist in their protection and management. I believe that such an initiative can add a new dimension to international cooperation.

I am directing the Secretary of the Interior, in coordination with the Council on Environmental Quality, and under the foreign policy guidance of the Secretary of State, to develop initiatives for presentation in appropriate international forums to further the objective of a World Heritage Trust.

Confronted with the pressures of population and development, and with the world's tremendously increased capacity for environmental modification, we must act together now to save for future generations the most outstanding natural areas as well as places of unique historical, archeological, architectural, and cultural values to mankind.

The president's words are a call to action. Such areas are in jeopardy because of lack of knowledge about the values at stake, because of inadequate facilities or services for managing these areas, or because of public and official apathy and indifference.

The danger is accentuated by the fact that once these resources have been materially changed or destroyed, they cannot be recovered. Unlike many environmental problems, which can often be cured or improved by willingness to spend money on improvement or abatement, these resources are truly irreplaceable.

What kind of resources do we mean?

I have already mentioned the Grand Canyon and the Serengeti Plains of East Africa. Others might be Angel Falls in South America, the Galapagos Islands with their unique fauna, and the habitats supporting rare and spectacular animal species such as the Indian rhinoceros, the tiger and the mountain gorilla. Such splendid areas exert influences on science, on human thought and culture, which extend far beyond the confines of their geographical position.

Other examples of historical and cultural sites might

include the pyramids, the Acropolis, Troy, Petra, the Roman Forum, Angkor Wat, Stonehenge, Abu Simbel, the Taj Mahal and Machu Picchu.

Current efforts to preserve and manage many of these sites are only national in scope. So the results vary greatly from country to country, depending upon such factors as recognition of the importance of the sites, local administrative and management capabilities, facilities, trained personnel, and the availability of funds.

In many developing countries, urgent needs to boost food production and industrial development, coupled with the importance of upgrading public health and education, often relegate the protection of important natural areas and cultural sites to a low position in the pecking order of government priorities. And in many countries, adequate technical and administrative organizations, skills and facilities simply do not exist. There are few or no opportunities to train professional personnel, and not enough money or technical advisors from foreign countries to offset the difference.

But along with the danger that natural areas and cultural sites will be ignored or severely damaged, there also comes a very favorable occasion—a rare opportunity for these nations to act together *now*—to save these resources both for ourselves and for the future.

Let us take a look at some of the key points which I think an international convention setting up the World Heritage Trust should contain.

First, the convention should contain a declaration that certain areas and sites are of universal significance and belong to the heritage of all mankind. It should point out that since these areas and sites are being threatened by the pressures of population growth, economic developments, and environmental changes, a new institution—the World Heritage ˙Trust—is being established to stimulate, promote and undertake international efforts to identify, protect, manage and preserve them.

One of the functions of the organization that administers the Heritage Trust would be to establish standards and criteria for areas to be included.

"Natural areas," for example, might well include areas of outstanding interest and value as a result of their unique or otherwise significant geology, physiography, flora or fauna. These should include areas which constitute important examples of natural ecosystems of special interest to science, areas containing a natural landscape of great beauty, and areas of importance to wildlife conservation and education.

Historic or cultural sites might be defined as sites that reflect significant events or states in the development of world civilization, including sites of major anthropological, archaeological, architectural and historic importance to the cultural history of mankind.

To assure efficiency of operation, quick responsiveness, and high professional caliber, the trust should be run on a day-to-day basis by a small body of experts, who would be selected by the representatives of the states signing the convention. This group would establish criteria to determine whether a specific area or site qualifies for recognition as a unit of the trust. It should also compile an inventory, based on inventories submitted by signatory states and on its own surveys, identifying areas and sites throughout the world which might qualify for inclusion in what could be called a World Heritage Register. I believe that the effort and discipline involved in developing such an inventory could have a major influence on public policy toward the environment throughout the world. The very fact that the nations of the world would be acting in concert to identify important areas would be a powerful force in building recognition of their value.

Once an area or site was inscribed in the register, it would become a matter of international concern to the signatory states, although, of course, the sovereign rights of the country in which it was located would in no way be infringed.

The convention should further specify that the representatives of the signatory nations should meet at suitable intervals to review the operations of the trust and to recommend any needed changes.

Since funds are required to accomplish the goals of the trust, a fund should be established for the identification, management, protection, and preservation of areas and sites included in the register. There are various ways in which money might be obtained for these purposes, but it seems proper that voluntary contributions should be solicited from the signatory states, from governmental and nongovernmental organizations, and from private foundations and individuals. Contributions could be made to the general fund or could be earmarked for special purposes. However, it should be emphasized that the World Heritage Trust is one international proposal where a maximum could be accomplished with very modest funding.

The professional staff of the trust should also evaluate requests from signatory states for technical and financial assistance. It should help establish standards for the management, protection, and preservation of areas and sites in the register, and should notify the representatives of the signatory states should corrective action be necessary.

Finally, the staff should cooperate fully with other governmental and nongovernmental organizations that are working toward similar objectives.

The states signing the convention should agree to undertake several steps. Most importantly, they must provide for the effective management, protection, and continuing preservation of registered areas and sites, in accordance with the standards established by the trust. This might well involve the enactment and enforcement of appropriate legislation or other action, and the signing of agreements between neighboring countries in cases of contiguous sites along international boundaries. Thus, we see world-wide upgrading of management of such areas as an important by-product of the trust agreement.

These, I think, are some of the main provisions a viable World Heritage Trust convention should contain. The whole world will profit from the identification, proper management, and continuing preservation of registered areas and sites. Signatory states will profit from the technical and financial assistance the trust will be able to offer. Moreover, they are virtually certain to profit as well from increased international tourism to these locations.

I know that the scheme which I have described may well fall short of perfection. Some will feel that it does not go far enough in providing protection and funding. Others will feel that it goes too far in dealing with a subject which should be left entirely to national decision. In my view, the World Heritage Trust as I have outlined it is a practical, effective step that can be taken now. Once the concept is established and accepted, then we can improve it and build on it, as experience indicates.

It is not the technical details, however, or even the actual working mechanisms of the World Heritage Trust, which are the crucial thing. It is the simple and yet revolutionary concept that throughout the world there exist natural and cultural areas of such unique value that they truly are part of the heritage, not only of individual nations, but of all mankind. That is the real heart of the matter. It is an idea which challenges the spirit. It is an idea which gives eloquent expression through cooperative international action to the truth that the earth is indeed man's home and belongs to us all.

It is an idea whose time has come.

Appendices

APPENDIX A

COMPLETE TEXT
OF THE WILDERNESS ACT

Public Law 88-577
88th Congress, S. 4
September 3, 1964

An Act

To establish a National Wilderness Preservation System for the permanent good of the whole people, and for other purposes.

Be it enacted by the Senate and House of Representatives of the United States of America in Congress assembled,

SHORT TITLE

SECTION I. This Act may be cited as the "Wilderness Act."

WILDERNESS SYSTEM ESTABLISHED—STATEMENT OF POLICY

SECTION 2. (a) In order to assure that an increasing population, accompanied by expanding settlement and growing mechanization, does not occupy and modify all areas within the United States and its possessions, leaving no lands designated for preservation and protection in their natural condition, it is hereby declared to be the policy of the Congress to secure for the American people of present and future generations the benefits of an enduring resource of wilderness. For this purpose there is hereby established a National Wilderness Preservation System to be composed of federally owned areas designated by Congress as "wilderness areas", and these shall be administered for the use and enjoyment of the American people in such manner as will leave them unimpaired for future use and enjoyment as wilderness, and so as to provide for the protection of these areas, the preservation of their wilderness character, and for the gathering and dissemination of information regarding their use and enjoyment as wilderness; and no Federal lands shall be designated as "wilderness areas" except as provided for in this Act or by a subsequent Act.

(b) The inclusion of an area in the National Wilderness Preservation System notwithstanding, the area shall continue to be managed by the Department and agency having jurisdiction thereover immediately before its inclusion in the National Wilderness Preservation System unless otherwise provided by Act of Congress. No appropriation shall be available for the payment of expenses or salaries for the administration of the National Wilderness Preservation System as a separate unit nor shall any appropriations be available for additional personnel stated as being required solely for the purpose of managing or administering areas solely because they are included within the National Wilderness Preservation System.

DEFINITION OF WILDERNESS

(c) A wilderness, in contrast with those areas where man and his own works dominate the landscape, is hereby recognized as an area where the earth and its community of life are untrammeled by man, where man himself is a visitor who does not remain. An area of wilderness is further defined to mean in this Act an area of undeveloped Federal land retaining its primeval character and influence, without permanent improvements or human habitation, which is protected and managed so as to preserve its natural conditions and which (1) generally appears to have been affected primarily by the forces of nature, with the imprint of man's work substantially unnoticeable; (2) has outstanding opportunities for solitude or a primitive and unconfined type of recreation; (3) has at least five thousand acres of land or is of sufficient size as to make practicable its preservation and use in an unimpaired condition; and (4) may also contain ecological, geological, or other features of scientific, educational, scenic, or historical value.

NATIONAL WILDERNESS PRESERVATION SYSTEM—
EXTENT OF SYSTEM

SECTION 3. (a) All areas within the national forests classified at least 30 days before the effective date of this Act by the

Secretary of Agriculture or the Chief of the Forest Service as "wilderness," "wild," or "canoe" are hereby designated as wilderness areas. The Secretary of Agriculture shall—

(1) Within one year after the effective date of this Act, file a map and legal description of each wilderness area with the Interior and Insular Affairs Committees of the United States Senate and the House of Representatives, and such descriptions shall have the same force and effect as if included in this Act: *Provided, however,* That correction of clerical and typographical errors in such legal descriptions and maps may be made.

(2) Maintain, available to the public, records pertaining to said wilderness areas, including maps and legal descriptions, copies of regulations governing them, copies of public notices of, and reports submitted to Congress regarding pending additions, eliminations, or modifications. Maps, legal descriptions, and regulations pertaining to wilderness areas within their respective jurisdictions also shall be available to the public in the offices of regional foresters, national forest supervisors, and forest rangers.

Classification. (b) The Secretary of Agriculture shall, within ten years after the enactment of this Act, review, as to its suitability or non-suitability for preservation as wilderness, each area in the national forests classified on the effective date of this Act by the Secretary of Agriculture or the Chief of the Forest Service as "primitive" and report his findings to the President.

Presidential recommendation to Congress. The President shall advise the United States Senate and House of Representatives of his recommendations with respect to the designation as "wilderness" or other reclassification of each area on which review has been completed, together with maps and a definition of boundaries. Such advice shall be given with respect to not less than one-third of all the areas now classified as "primitive" within three years after the enactment of this Act, not less than two-thirds within seven years after the enactment of this Act, and the remaining areas within ten years after the enactment of this Act.

Congressional approval. Each recommendation of the President for designation as "wilderness" shall become effective only if so provided by an Act of Congress. Areas classified as "primitive" on the effective date of this Act shall continue to be administered under the rules and regulations affecting such areas on the

effective date of this Act until Congress has determined otherwise. Any such area may be increased in size by the President at
the time he submits his recommendations to the Congress by not
more than five thousand acres with no more than one thousand
two hundred and eighty acres of such increase in any one compact unit; if it is proposed to increase the size of any such area by
more than five thousand acres or by more than one thousand two
hundred and eighty acres in any one compact unit the increase in
size shall not become effective until acted upon by Congress.
Nothing herein contained shall limit the President in proposing, as
part of his recommendations to Congress, the alteration of existing boundaries of primitive areas or recommending the addition
of any contiguous area of national forest lands predominantly of
wilderness value. Notwithstanding any other provisions of this
Act, the Secretary of Agriculture may complete his review and
delete such area as may be necessary, but not to exceed seven
thousand acres, from the southern tip of the Gore Range-Eagles
Nest Primitive Area, Colorado, if the Secretary determines that
such action is in the public interest.

Report to President. (c) Within ten years after the effective
date of this Act the Secretary of the Interior shall review every
roadless area of five thousand contiguous acres or more in the
national parks, monuments and other units of the national park
system and every such area of, and every roadless island within,
the national wildlife refuges and game ranges, under his jurisdiction on the effective date of this Act and shall report to the
President his recommendation as to the suitability or non-suitability of each such area or island for preservation as wilderness.

Presidential recommendation to Congress. The President shall
advise the President of the Senate and the Speaker of the House
of Representatives of his recommendation with respect to the
designation as wilderness of each such area or island on which
review has been completed, together with a map thereof and a
definition of its boundaries. Such advice shall be given with respect to not less than one-third of the areas and islands to be
reviewed under this subsection within three years after enactment
of this Act, not less than two-thirds within seven years of enactment of this Act, and the remainder within ten years of enactment of this Act.

Congressional approval. A recommendation of the President
for designation as wilderness shall become effective only if so
provided by an Act of Congress. Nothing contained herein shall,
by implication or otherwise, be construed to lessen the present

statutory authority of the Secretary of the Interior with respect to the maintenance of roadless areas within units of the national park system.

Suitability. (d) (1) The Secretary of Agriculture and the Secretary of the Interior shall, prior to submitting any recommendations to the President with respect to the suitability of any area for preservation as wilderness—

Publication in Federal Register. (A) give such public notice of the proposed action as they deem appropriate, including publication in the Federal Register and in a newspaper having general circulation in the area or areas in the vicinity of the affected land;

Hearings. (B) hold a public hearing or hearings at a location or locations convenient to the area affected. The hearings shall be announced through such means as the respective Secretaries involved deem appropriate, including notices in the Federal Register and in newspapers of general circulation in the area: *Provided.* That if the lands involved are located in more than one State, at least one hearing shall be held in each State in which a portion of the land lies;

(C) at least thirty days before the date of a hearing advise the Governor of each State and the governing board of each county, or in Alaska the borough, in which the lands are located, and Federal departments and agencies concerned, and invite such officials and Federal agencies to submit their views on the proposed action at the hearing or by no later than thirty days following the date of the hearing.

(2) Any views submitted to the appropriate Secretary under the provisions of (1) of this subsection with respect to any area shall be included with any recommendations to the President and to Congress with respect to such area.

Proposed modification. (e) Any modification or adjustment of boundaries of any wilderness area shall be recommended by the appropriate Secretary after public notice of such proposal and public hearing or hearings as provided in subsection (d) of this section. The proposed modification or adjustment shall them be recommended with map and description thereof to the President. The President shall advise the United States Senate and the House of Representatives of his recommendations with respect to such modification or adjustment and such recommendations shall become effective only in the same manner as provided for in subsections (b) and (c) of this section.

USE OF WILDERNESS AREAS

SECTION 4. (a) The purposes of this Act are hereby declared to be within and supplemental to the purposes for which national forests and units of the national park and wildlife refuge systems are established and administered and—

(1) Nothing in this Act shall be deemed to be in interference with the purpose for which national forests are established as set forth in the Act of June 4, 1897 (30 Stat. 11), and the Multiple-Use Sustained-Yield Act of June 12, 1960 (74 Stat. 215).

(2) Nothing in this Act shall modify the restrictions and provisions of the Shipstead-Nolan Act (Public Law 539, Seventy-first Congress, July 10, 1930; 46 Stat. 1020), the Thye-Blatnik Act (Public Law 733, Eightieth Congress, June 22, 1948; 62 Stat. 568), and the Humphrey-Thye-Blatnik-Andresen Act (Public Law 607, Eighty-fourth Congress, June 22, 1956; 70 Stat. 326), as applying to the Superior National Forest or the regulations of the Secretary of Agriculture.

(3) Nothing in this Act shall modify the statutory authority under which units of the national park system are created. Further, the designation of any area of any park, monument, or other unit of the national park system as a wilderness area pursuant to this Act shall in no manner lower the standards evolved for the use and preservation of such park, monument, or other unit of the national park system in accordance with the Act of August 25, 1916, the statutory authority under which the area was created, or any other Act of Congress which might pertain to or affect such area, including, but not limited to, the Act of June 8, 1906 (34 Stat. 225; 16 U.S.C. 432 et seq.); section 3(2) of the Federal Power Act (16 U.S.C. 796(2)); and the Act of August 21, 1935 (49 Stat. 666; 16 U.S.C. 461 et seq.).

(b) Except as otherwise provided in this Act, each agency administering any area designated as wilderness shall be responsible for preserving the wilderness character of the area and shall so administer such area for such other purposes for which it may have been established as also to preserve its wilderness character.

Except as otherwise provided in this Act, wilderness areas shall be devoted to the public purposes of recreational, scenic, scientific, educational, conservation, and historical use.

PROHIBITION OF CERTAIN USES

(c) Except as specifically provided for in this Act, and subject to existing private rights, there shall be no commercial enterprise and no permanent road within any wilderness area designated by this Act and, except as necessary to meet minimum requirements for the administration of the area for the purpose of this Act (including measures required in emergencies involving the health and safety of persons within the area), there shall be no temporary road, no use of motor vehicles, motorized equipment or motorboats, no landing of aircraft, no other form of mechanical transport, and no structure or installation within any such area.

SPECIAL PROVISIONS

(d) The following special provisions are hereby made:

(1) Within wilderness areas designated by this Act the use of aircraft or motorboats, where these uses have already become established, may be permitted to continue subject to such restrictions as the Secretary of Agriculture deems desirable. In addition, such measures may be taken as may be necessary in the control of fire, insects, and diseases, subject to such conditions as the Secretary deems desirable.

(2) Nothing in this Act shall prevent within national forest wilderness areas any activity, including prospecting, for the purpose of gathering information about mineral or other resources, if such activity is carried on in a manner compatible with the preservation of the wilderness environment. Furthermore, in accordance with such program as the Secretary of the Interior shall develop and conduct in consultation with the Secretary of Agriculture, such areas shall be surveyed on a planned, recurring basis consistent with the concept of wilderness preservation by the Geological Survey and the Bureau of Mines to determine the mineral values, if any, that may be present; and the results of such surveys shall be made available to the public and submitted to the President and Congress.

Mineral leases, claims, etc. (3) Notwithstanding any other provisions of this Act, until midnight December 31, 1983, the United States mining laws and all laws pertaining to mineral leasing shall, to the same extent as applicable prior to the effective date of this Act, extend to those national forest lands designated by this Act as "wilderness areas"; subject, however, to such reasonable regulations governing ingress and egress as may be prescribed by the Secretary of Agriculture consistent with the use of the land for mineral location and development and exploration, drilling, and production, and use of land for transmission lines, waterlines, telephone lines, or facilities necessary in exploring, drilling, producing, mining, and processing operations, including where essential the use of mechanized ground or air equipment and restoration as near as practicable of the surface of the land disturbed in performing prospecting, location, and, in oil and gas leasing, discovery work, exploration, drilling, and production, as soon as they have served their purpose. Mining locations lying within the boundaries of said wilderness areas shall be held and used solely for mining or processing operations and uses reasonably incident thereto; and hereafter, subject to valid existing rights, all patents issued under the mining laws of the United States affecting national forest lands designated by this Act as wilderness areas shall convey title to the mineral deposits within the claim, together with the right to cut and use so much of the mature timber therefrom as may be needed in the extraction, removal, and beneficiation of the mineral deposits, if the timber is not otherwise reasonably available, and if the timber is cut under sound principles of forest management as defined by the national forest rules and regulations, but each such patent shall reserve to the United States all title in or to the surface of the lands and products thereof, and no use of the surface of the claim or the resources therefrom not reasonably required for carrying on mining or prospecting shall be allowed except as otherwise expressly provided in this Act: *Provided*, That, unless hereafter specifically authorized, no patent within wilderness areas designated by this Act shall issue after December 31, 1983, except for the valid claims existing on or before December 31, 1983. Mining claims located after the effective date of this Act within the boundaries of wilderness areas designated by this Act shall create no rights in excess of those rights which may be patented under the provisions of this subsection. Mineral leases, permits, and licenses covering lands within national forest wilderness areas designated by this Act shall contain such reasonable stipulations as may be prescribed by the Secretary of Agriculture for the protection of the wilderness character of the land consistent with the use of the land for the purposes for which they are leased, permitted, or licensed. Subject to valid rights then existing, effective January 1, 1984, the minerals in lands designated by this Act as wilderness areas are withdrawn from all forms of appropriation under the mining laws and from disposition under all laws pertaining to mineral leasing and all amendments thereto.

Water resources. (4) Within wilderness areas in the national forests designated by this Act, (1) the President may, within a specific area and in accordance with such regulations as he may deem desirable, authorize prospecting for water resources, the establishment and maintenance of reservoirs, water-conservation works, power projects, transmission lines, and other facilities needed in the public interest, including the road construction and maintenance essential to development and use thereof, upon his determination that such use or uses in the specific area will better serve the interests of the United States and the people thereof than will its denial; and (2) the grazing of livestock, where established prior to the effective date of this Act, shall be permitted to continue subject to such reasonable regulations as are deemed necessary by the Secretary of Agriculture.

(5) Other provisions of this Act to the contrary notwithstanding, the management of the Boundary Waters Canoe Area, formerly designated as the Superior, Little Indian Sioux, and Caribou Roadless Areas, in the Superior National Forest, Minnesota, shall be in accordance with regulations established by the Secretary of Agriculture in accordance with the general purpose of maintaining, without unnecessary restrictions on other uses, including that of timber, the primitive character of the area, particularly in the vicinity of lakes, streams, and portages: *Provided,* That nothing in this Act shall preclude the continuance within the area of any already established use of motorboats.

(6) Commercial services may be performed within the wilderness areas designated by this Act to the extent necessary for activities which are proper for realizing the recreational or other wilderness purposes of the areas.

(7) Nothing in this Act shall constitute an express or implied claim or denial on the part of the Federal Government as to exemption from State water laws.

(8) Nothing in this Act shall be construed as affecting the jurisdiction or responsibilities of the several States with respect to wildlife and fish in the national forests.

STATE AND PRIVATE LANDS WITHIN WILDERNESS AREAS

SECTION 5. (a) In any case where State-owned or privately owned land is completely surrounded by national forest lands within areas designated by this Act as wilderness, such State or private owner shall be given such rights as may be necessary to assure adequate access to such State-owned or privately owned land by such State or private owner and their successors in interest, or the State-owned land or privately owned land shall be exchanged for federally owned land in the same State of approximately equal value under authorities available to the Secretary of Agriculture:

Transfers, restriction. Provided, however, That the United States shall not transfer to a State or private owner any mineral interests unless the State or private owner relinquishes or causes to be relinquished to the United States the mineral interest in the surrounded land.

(b) In any case where valid mining claims or other valid occupancies are wholly within a designated national forest wilderness area, the Secretary of Agriculture shall, by reasonable regulations consistent with the preservation of the area as wilderness, permit ingress and egress to such surrounded areas by means which have been or are being customarily enjoyed with respect to other such areas similarly situated.

Acquisition. (c) Subject to the appropriation of funds by Congress, the Secretary of Agriculture is authorized to acquire privately owned land within the perimeter of any area designated by this Act as wilderness if (1) the owner concurs in such acquisition or (2) the acquisition is specifically authorized by Congress.

GIFTS, BEQUESTS, AND CONTRIBUTIONS

SECTION 6. (a) The Secretary of Agriculture may accept gifts or bequests of land within wilderness areas designated by this Act for preservation as wilderness. The Secretary of Agriculture may also accept gifts or bequests of land adjacent to wilderness areas designated by this Act for preservation as wilderness if he has given sixty days advance notice thereof to the President of the Senate and the Speaker of the House of Representatives. Land accepted by the Secretary of Agriculture under this section shall become part of the wilderness area involved. Regulations with regard to any such land may be in accordance with such agreements, consistent with the policy of this Act, as are made at the time of such gift, or such conditions, consistent with such policy, as may be included in, and accepted with, such bequest.

(b) The Secretary of Agriculture or the Secretary of the Interior is authorized to accept private contributions and gifts to be used to further the purposes of this Act.

ANNUAL REPORTS

SECTION 7. At the opening of each session of Congress, the Secretaries of Agriculture and Interior shall jointly report to the President for transmission to Congress on the status of the wilderness system, including a list and descriptions of the areas in the system, regulations in effect, and other pertinent information, together with any recommendations they may care to make.

Approved September 3, 1964.

LEGISLATIVE HISTORY:

HOUSE REPORTS:
   No. 1538 accompanying H. R. 9070 (Committee on Interior & Insular Affairs) and No. 1829 (Committee of Conference).

SENATE REPORT:
   No. 109 (Committee on Interior & Insular Affairs).

CONGRESSIONAL RECORD:
   Vol. 109 (1963):
      April 4, 8, considered in Senate.
      April 9, considered and passed Senate.
   Vol. 110 (1964):
      July 28, considered in House.
      July 30, considered and passed House, amended, in lieu of H. R. 9070.
      August 20, House and Senate agreed to conference report.

APPENDIX B

PRESENT AND POTENTIAL UNITS OF THE NATIONAL WILDERNESS PRESERVATION SYSTEM*

(January 1, 1972)

Starting in 1929, the Forest Service established Primitive Areas within National Forests. Starting in 1939, Wilderness and Wild Areas were administratively designated by the Secretary of Agriculture from within these Primitive Areas to be managed and protected to preserve their wilderness values. Wilderness Areas were defined as 100,000 acres or more. Wild Areas were smaller, but over 5,000 acres.

Upon passage of the Wilderness Act, several changes took place. The term Wild Area was dropped and the areas that had been designated as Wilderness and Wild were both called Wilderness and became the nucleus of the National Wilderness Preservation System. The Primitive Areas, in accordance with the Law, were made subject to further study, public hearing, recommendations to Congress, and a decision by Congress in each case as to whether or not the area would be added to the National Wilderness Preservation System as a Wilderness, and if so what its boundaries would be.

The Wilderness Act also made the term Wilderness applicable to the roadless areas of the lands under the jurisdiction of the National Park Service and the wildlife refuges and ranges. Such lands would go through the same process as National Forest Primitive Areas to determine whether or not they will become part of the National Wilderness Preservation System.

After the Secretary of Agriculture makes his recommendation to the President, and the President to Congress, and Congress has authorized the establishment of a wilderness area, the term Primi-

*Compiled by The Wilderness Society

tive Area is no longer applied. However, the Bureau of Land Management in the Department of the Interior is using that term in administratively designating for special management lands of a wilderness character under its jurisdiction. The Wilderness Law does not apply to these BLM lands.

National Park Service and Bureau of Sport Fisheries and Wildlife proposals for wilderness designation have frequently involved the "splitting" of larger administrative units to form two or more separate Wildernesses.

The National Wildlife Refuges and Ranges of the Bureau of Sport Fisheries and Wildlife vary widely as to acreage. In some cases a definite figure cannot be given because of shifting island boundaries.

The term "de facto wilderness" applies to lands of a wilderness character which have not been reviewed under the terms of the Wilderness Act or proposed for inclusion in the Wilderness System by the administering agency. They may be the subject of legislation introduced by Congressional delegations in response to the demand of constituents. They may have undergone agency reviews and been excluded from the President's proposal. Or they may be newly defined wild land units that can be established as wilderness areas by Congress at any time, with or without prior agency reviews. In all cases, the Congressional prerogative—to give this protection under the Wilderness Law or to remove it—remains in force. Some of these de facto areas which have been proposed for addition to the National Wilderness Preservation System are shown in footnotes to the following tables.

In these tables the figures represent the agencies' gross acreage for each unit listed. Since "net" figures are available only for National Forest candidate areas, the gross acreage figure was used to give a consistent picture of the wilderness acreage now being considered for inclusion in the Wilderness System. Grand total for each state shows approximate acreage under different agencies.

Abbreviations: NM-National Monument; NP-National Park; NWR-National Wildlife Refuge; PA-(National Forest) Primitive Area; FS-Forest Service; NPS-National Park Service; BSFW-Bureau of Sport Fisheries and Wildlife.

Name of Area	Placed in NWPS (date) (acres)	Under Review by Agency or Congress (approx. acres)

ALABAMA[1]

[1]**Sipsey Wilderness** (proposed) 12,000 acres in Bankhead N.F., introduced in Congress without agency proposal.

ALASKA

Name of Area	Placed in NWPS (date) (acres)	Under Review (approx. acres)
Aleutian Islands N.W.R.		2,720,430
Arctic N.W.R.		8,899,859
Bering Sea N.W.R. (1970)	41,113	
Bogoslof N.W.R. (1970)	390	
Cape Newenham N.W.R.		265,000
Chamisso N.W.R.		455
Clarence Rhode N.W. Range		1,870,015
Forrester Island N.W.R. (1970)	2,630	
Glacier Bay N.M.		2,803,840
Hazen Bay N.W.R.		6,800
Hazy Islands N.W.R. (1970)	42	
Izembek N.W.R.		415,015
Katmai N.M.		2,792,137
Kenai National Moose Range		1,730,000
Kodiak N.W.R.		1,815,000
Mount McKinley N.P.		1,939,493
Nunivak N.W.R.		1,109,384
St. Lazaria Island N.W.R. (1970)	62	
Semidi N.W.R.		8,422
Simeonof N.W.R.		25,271
Tuxedni N.W.R. (1970)	6,402	
TOTAL:	50,639	26,401,121

Agencies: 3 NPS 7,535,470 + 18 BSFW 18,916,290

TOTAL—ALASKA   **26,451,760**

Name of Area	Placed in NWPS (date) (acres)	Under Review by Agency or Congress (approx. acres)
ARIZONA		
Blue Range P.A. (also in New Mexico)		181,566
Cabeza Prieta Game Range		860,000
Canyon de Chelly N.M.		83,840
Chiricahua N.M.		10,645
Chiricahua Wilderness (1964)	18,000	
Galiuro Wilderness (1964)	52,717	
Glen Canyon National Recreation Area		1,196,545
Grand Canyon N.M.		198,280
Grand Canyon N.P.		673,575
Havasu Lake N.W.R. (includes California acreage)		41,494
Imperial N.W.R. (includes California acreage)		25,764
Kofa Game Range		660,000
Lake Mead National Recreation Area (also in Nevada)		1,217,832
Mazatzal Wilderness (1964)	205,346	
Mount Baldy Wilderness (1970)	7,000	
Organ Pipe Cactus N.M.		330,874
Petrified Forest N.P. (1970)	50,260	
Pine Mountain P.A.		16,399
Saguaro N.M.		78,084
Sierra Ancha Wilderness (1964)	20,850	
Superstition Wilderness (1964)	124,140	
Sycamore Canyon P.A.		49,590
Wupatki N.M.		35,233
TOTAL:	478,313	5,659,721

Agencies: 9FS 675,608 + 10NPS 3,875,168 + 4BSFW 1,587,258

TOTAL—ARIZONA   **6,138,034**

Name of Area	Placed in NWPS (date) (acres)	Under Review by Agency or Congress (approx. acres)

ARKANSAS

Name of Area	Placed in NWPS (date) (acres)	Under Review by Agency or Congress (approx. acres)
White River N.W.R.		112,399
TOTAL:		112,399

Agencies: 1 BSFW 112,399

TOTAL—ARKANSAS   **112,399**

CALIFORNIA[1,2,3]

Name of Area	Placed in NWPS (date) (acres)	Under Review by Agency or Congress (approx. acres)
Agua Tibia P.A.		26,760
Caribou Wilderness (1964)	19,080	
Cucamonga Wilderness (1964)	9,022	
Death Valley N.M. (includes Nevada acreage)		1,907,760
Desolation Wilderness (1969)	41,343	
Dome Land Wilderness (1964)	62,561	
Emigrant Basin P.A.		97,020
Farallon N.W.R.		141
Havasu Lake N.W.R. (see Arizona)		—
High Sierra P.A.		10,247
Hoover Wilderness (1964)	42,800	
Imperial N.W.R. (see Arizona)		—
John Muir Wilderness (1964)	504,263	
Joshua Tree N.M.		588,184
Kings Canyon N.P.		460,331
Lassen Volcanic N.P.	106,934	

[1] **Granite Chief Wilderness** (proposed) 36,000 acres in Tahoe N.F., introduced in Congress without agency proposal.

[2] **San Joachin Wilderness** (proposed) 43,000 acres in Sierra and Inyo National Forests, introduced in Congress without agency proposal.

[3] **Siskiyou Wilderness** (proposed) 153,000 acres in Siskiyou, Six Rivers, and Klamath National Forests, introduced in Congress without agency proposal.

Name of Area	Placed in NWPS (date) (acres)	Under Review by Agency or Congress (approx. acres)
Lava Beds N.M.		46,239
Marble Mountain Wilderness (1964)	214,543	
Minarets Wilderness (1964)	109,559	
Mokclumne Wilderness (1964)	50,400	
Pinnacles N.M.		14,498
Point Reyes National Seashore		64,546
Salmon Trinity Alps P.A.		223,340
San Gabriel Wilderness (1968)	36,137	
San Gorgonio Wilderness (1964)	34,718	
San Jacinto Wilderness (1964)	21,955	
San Rafael Wilderness (1968)	142,918	
Sequoia N.P.		386,863
South Warner Wilderness (1964)	69,547	
Thousand Lakes Wilderness (1964)	16,335	
Ventana Wilderness (1969)	54,857	
Yolla-Bolly Middle Eel Wilderness (1964)	111,091	
Yosemite N.P.		761,320
TOTAL:	1,541,129	4,694,183

Agencies: 21 FS 1,898,496 + 9 NPS 4,336,675 + 3 BSFW 141

TOTAL—CALIFORNIA	**6,235,312**

COLORADO[1]

Black Canyon of the Gunnison N.M.	13,667
Colorado N.M.	17,660
Dinosaur N.M. (see acreage in Utah)	—
Flat Tops P.A.	102,124
Gore Range-Eagles Nest P.A.	61,275
Great Sands Dunes N.M.	36,740

[1] Indian Peaks Wilderness (proposed) 75,000 acres in Roosevelt and Arapahoe National Forests, introduced in Congress without agency proposal.

Name of Area	Placed in NWPS (date) (acres)	Under Review by Agency or Congress (approx. acres)
La Garita Wilderness (1964)	48,486	
Maroon Bells-Snowmass Wilderness (1964)	71,329	
Mesa Verde N.P.		52,074
Mount Zirkel Wilderness (1964)	72,472	
Rawah Wilderness (1964)	26,674	
Rocky Mountain N.P.		262,191
San Juan P.A. (Weminuche)		240,000
Uncompagre P.A.		69,253
Upper Rio Grande P.A. (Weminuche)		56,600
West Elk Wilderness (1964)	61,412	
Wilson Mountains P.A.		27,347
TOTAL:	280,373	1,938,931

Agencies: 11 FS 836,972 + 6 NPS 382,332

TOTAL—COLORADO   **1,219,304**

FLORIDA

Name of Area	Placed in NWPS (date) (acres)	Under Review by Agency or Congress (approx. acres)
Caloosahatchee N.W.R.		40
Cedar Keys N.W.R.		378
Chassahowitzka N.W.R.		28,995
Everglades N.P.		1,400,533
Great White Heron N.W.R.		1,997
Island Bay N.W.R. (1970)	20	
Key West N.W.R.		2,019
Matlacha N.W.R.		10
National Key Deer W.R.		7,306
Passage Key N.W.R. (1970)	20	
Pelican Island N.W.R. (1970)	3	

Name of Area	Placed in NWPS (date) (acres)	Under Review by Agency or Congress (approx. acres)
Pine Island N.W.R.		31
St. Marks N.W.R.		65,136
TOTAL:	43	1,506,445

Agencies: 1 NPS 1,400,533 + 12 BSFW 105,955

TOTAL—FLORIDA		**1,506,488**

GEORGIA

Blackbeard Island N.W.R.		5,618
Okefenokee N.W.R.		319,000
Piedmont N.W.R.		33,676
Tybee N.W.R.		100
Wolf Island N.W.R.		538
TOTAL:		358,922

Agencies: 5 BSFW 358,922

TOTAL—GEORGIA		**358,922**

HAWAII

Haleakala N.P.		27,283
Hawaii Volcanoes N.P.		220,345
Hawaiian Islands N.W.R.		1,765
TOTAL:		249,393

Agencies: 2 NPS 247,628 + 1 BSFW 1,765

TOTAL—HAWAII		**249,393**

Name of Area	Placed in NWPS (date) (acres)	Under Review by Agency or Congress (approx. acres)

IDAHO[1]

Name of Area	Placed in NWPS (date) (acres)	Under Review by Agency or Congress (approx. acres)
Craters of the Moon N.M. (1970)	43,243	
Deer Flat N.W.R.		11,586
Idaho P.A.		1,232,744
Salmon River Breaks P.A.		217,185
Sawtooth P.A.		200,942
Selway-Bitterroot Wilderness (see also Montana) (1964)	989,179	
Yellowstone N.P. (see also Montana and Wyoming)	—	31,488
TOTAL:	1,032,422	1,693,945

Agencies: 4 FS 2,640,050 + 2 NPS 74,731 + 1 BSFW 11,586

TOTAL—IDAHO   **2,726,367**

[1]**Upper Selway Wilderness** (proposed) 250,000 acres in Bitterroot and Nez Perce National Forests, introduced in Congress without agency proposal.

ILLINOIS

Name of Area		Under Review by Agency or Congress (approx. acres)
Mark Twain N.W.F. Islands (see also Iowa, Minnesota, Missouri, Wisconsin)		14,680
Upper Mississippi Wildlife and Fish Refuge (see also Iowa, Minnesota, Wisconsin)		23,260
TOTAL:		37,940

Agencies: 2 BSFW 37,940

TOTAL—ILLINOIS   **37,940**

Name of Area	Placed in NWPS (date) (acres)	Under Review by Agency or Congress (approx. acres)

IOWA

Mark Twain N.W.R. (see Illinois)		10,375
Upper Mississippi Wildlife and Fish Refuge (see also Illinois, Minnesota, Wisconsin)		50,637
TOTAL:		61,012

Agencies: 2 BSFW 61,012

TOTAL—IOWA   **61,012**

KENTUCKY

Cumberland Gap National Historical Park (see also Virginia and Tennessee)		10,686
Mammoth Cave N.P.		51,354
TOTAL:		62,040

Agencies: 2 NPS 62,040

TOTAL—KENTUCKY   **62,040**

LOUISIANA

Breton Island N.W.R.		9,047
Sabine N.W.R.		142,846
Shell Keys N.W.R.		8
TOTAL:		151,901

Agencies: 3 BSFW 151,901

TOTAL—LOUISIANA   **151,901**

Name of Area	Placed in NWPS (date) (acres)	Under Review by Agency or Congress (approx. acres)
MAINE		
Moosehorn N.W.R. (1970) (Edmunds unit and Birch Island unit)	2,782	
Baring unit		22,000
TOTAL:	2,782	22,000
Agencies: 1 BSFW 24,782		
TOTAL—MAINE		**24,782**
MARYLAND		
Martin N.W.R.		4,423
TOTAL:		4,423
Agencies: 1 BSFW 4,423		
TOTAL—MARYLAND		**4,423**
MASSACHUSETTS		
Monomoy Island N.W.R. (1970)	1,340	
TOTAL:	1,340	
Agencies: 1 BSFW 1,340		
TOTAL—MASSACHUSETTS		**1,340**

Name of Area	Placed in NWPS (date) (acres)	Under Review by Agency or Congress (approx. acres)
MICHIGAN		
Huron Islands N.W.R. (1970)	147	
Isle Royale N.P.		539,341
Michigan Islands N.W.R. (1970)	12	
Seney N.W.R. (1970)	25,150	
Sleeping Bear Dunes National Lakeshore		71,068
TOTAL:	25,309	610,409

Agencies: 1 NPS 539,341 + 4 BSFW 96,377

TOTAL—MICHIGAN 635,718

MINNESOTA		
Boundary Waters Canoe Area Wilderness (1964)	1,029,257	
Upper Mississippi Refuge Islands (see also Iowa, Illinois, Wisconsin)		33,225
TOTAL:	1,029,257	33,225

Agencies: 1 FS 1,029,257 + 1 BSFW 33,225

TOTAL—MINNESOTA 1,062,482

MISSISSIPPI		
Horn Island N.W.R.		2,442
Petit Bois N.W.R.		749
TOTAL:		3,191

Agencies: 2 BSFW 3,191

TOTAL—MISSISSIPPI 3,191

	Placed in NWPS (date) (acres)	*Under Review by Agency or Congress (approx. acres)*
Name of Area		

MISSOURI

Mark Twain N.W.R. (Islands) (see also Illinois, Iowa, Minnesota and Wisconsin) Mingo N.W.F.		21,646 232
TOTAL:		21,878

Agencies: 2 BSFW 21,878

TOTAL— MISSOURI		**21,878**

MONTANA[1,2]

Absaroka P.A.		64,000
Anaconda-Pintlar Wilderness (1964)	159,086	
Beartooth P.A.		230,000
Bob Marshall Wilderness (1964)	950,000	
Cabinet Mountains Wilderness (1964)	94,272	
Charles M. Russell National Wildlife Range		926,574
Gates of the Mountains Wilderness (1964)	28,562	
Glacier N.P.		1,013,127

[1] **Jewel Basin Wilderness** (proposed) 21,000 acres in Flathead N.F., introduced in Congress without agency proposal.

[2] **Lincoln-Scapegoat Wilderness** (proposed) 245,500 acres in Helena, Lewis & Clark and Lolo National Forests, introduced in Congress without agency proposal.

Name of Area	Placed in NWPS (date) (acres)	Under Review by Agency or Congress (approx. acres)
Mission Mountains P.A.		75,500
Red Rock Lakes Migratory Waterfowl Refuge		40,223
Selway-Bitterroot Wilderness (see Idaho) (1964)	254,480	
Spanish Peaks P.A.		50,776
Yellowstone N.P. (see also Idaho and Wyoming)		149,032
TOTAL:	1,486,400	2,549,232

Agencies: 9 FS 1,906,676 + 2 NPS 1,162,159 + 2 BSFW 966,797

TOTAL—MONTANA   **4,035,632**

NEBRASKA

Crescent Lake N.W.R.		45,996
Valentine N.W.R.		71,516
TOTAL:		117,512

Agencies: 2 BSFW 117,512

TOTAL—NEBRASKA   **117,512**

NEVADA

Anaho Island N.W.R.		248
Charles Sheldon Antelope Range		578,738
Death Valley N.M. (see California)		—
Desert National Wildlife Range		1,588,379

Name of Area	Placed in NWPS (date) (acres)	Under Review by Agency or Congress (approx. acres)
Jarbidge Wilderness (1964)	64,827	
Lake Mead National Recreation Area (see Arizona)		—
TOTAL:	64,827	2,859,852

Agencies: 1 FS 64,827 + 2 NPS 692,487 + 3 BSFW 2,167,365

TOTAL—NEVADA   **2,924,679**

NEW HAMPSHIRE

Great Gulf Wilderness (1964)	5,552	
TOTAL:	5,552	

Agencies: 1 FS 5,552

TOTAL—NEW HAMPSHIRE   **5,552**

NEW JERSEY

Brigantine N.W.R.		19,388
Great Swamp N.W.R. Wilderness (1968)	3,750	
TOTAL:	3,750	19,388

Agencies: 2 BSFW 23,138

TOTAL—NEW JERSEY   **23,138**

Name of Area	Placed in NWPS (date) (acres)	Under Review by Agency or Congress (approx. acres)
NEW MEXICO		
Bandelier N.M.		29,661
Black Range P.A.		169,984
Blue Range P.A. (see also Arizona)		36,598
Bosque del Apache N.W.R.		25,000
Carlsbad Caverns N.P.		46,753
Chaco Canyon N.M.		21,509
Gila P.A.		132,788
Gila Wilderness (1964)	433,916	
Pecos Wilderness (1964)	167,416	
Salt Creek Wilderness (1970)	8,500	
San Andres N.W.R.		57,217
San Pedro Parks Wilderness (1964)	41,132	
Wheeler Peak Wilderness (1964)	6,029	
White Mountain Wilderness (1964)	31,283	
White Sands N.M.		146,535
TOTAL:	688,276	666,045

Agencies: 8 FS 1,019,146 + 4 NPS 244,458 + 3 BSFW 90,717

TOTAL—NEW MEXICO		1,354,321

Name of Area	Placed in NWPS (date) (acres)	Under Review by Agency or Congress (approx. acres)
NORTH CAROLINA		
Great Smoky Mountains N.P. (see also Tennessee)		274,290
Linville Gorge Wilderness (1964)	7,575	
Shining Rock Wilderness (1964)	13,350	
TOTAL:	20,925	

Agencies: 2 FS 20,925 + 1 NPS 274,290

TOTAL—NORTH CAROLINA		295,215

Name of Area	Placed in NWPS (date) (acres)	Under Review by Agency or Congress (approx. acres)
NORTH DAKOTA		
Chase Lake N.W.F.		74,821
Lostwood N.W.F.		26,747
Theodore Roosevelt National Memorial Park		70,436
TOTAL:		172,004

Agencies: 1 NPS 70,436 + 2 BSFW 101,568

TOTAL—NORTH DAKOTA   **172,004**

OHIO		
West Sister Island N.W.R.		85
TOTAL:		85

Agencies: 1 BSFW 85

TOTAL—OHIO   **85**

OKLAHOMA		
Wichita Mountains National Refuge (1970)	8,900	
TOTAL:	8,900	

Agencies: 1 BSFW 8,900

TOTAL—OKLAHOMA   **8,900**

Name of Area	Placed in NWPS (date) (acres)	Under Review by Agency or Congress (approx. acres)
OREGON[1]		
Crater Lake N.P.		160,290
Diamond Peak Wilderness (1964)	35,440	
Eagle Cap Wilderness (1964)	221,355	
Gearhart Mountain Wilderness (1964)	18,709	
Hart Mountain National Antelope Refuge		47,000
Kalmiopsis Wilderness (1964)	76,900	
Klamath Forest N.W.R.		15,226
Malheur N.W.R.		49,000
Mount Hood Wilderness (1964)	14,160	
Mount Jefferson Wilderness (1968)	99,600	
Mount Washington Wilderness (1964)	46,655	
Mountain Lakes Wilderness (1964)	23,071	
Oregon Island N.W.R. Wilderness (1970)	21	367
Strawberry Mountain Wilderness (1964)	33,653	
Three Arch Rocks N.W.R. Wilderness (1970)	17	
Three Sisters Wilderness (1964)	196,708	
TOTAL:	766,289	271,883

Agencies: 10 FS 766,251 + 1 NPS 160,290 + 5 BSFW 111,631

TOTAL—OREGON   **1,038,172**

[1]**Minami River Wilderness** (proposed) 80,000 acres in Wallowa-Whitman National Forest, proposed as addition to Eagle Cap Wilderness.

Name of Area	Placed in NWPS (date) (acres)	Under Review by Agency or Congress (approx. acres)

SOUTH CAROLINA

Cape Romain N.W.R.		34,017
Carolina Sandhills N.W.R.		45,591
TOTAL:		79,608

Agencies: 2 BSFW 79,608

TOTAL—SOUTH CAROLINA   **79,608**

SOUTH DAKOTA

Badlands N.M.		243,505
TOTAL:		243,505

Agencies: 1 NPS 243,505

TOTAL—SOUTH DAKOTA   **243,505**

TENNESSEE

Cumberland Gap National Historical Park (see also Kentucky and Virginia)		2,007
Great Smoky Mountains N.P. (see also North Carolina)		239,768
TOTAL:		241,775

Agencies: 2 NPS 241,775

TOTAL—TENNESSEE   **241,775**

Name of Area	Placed in NWPS (date) (acres)	Under Review by Agency or Congress (approx. acres)

TEXAS

Big Bend N.P.		708,221
Laguna Atascosa N.W.R.		45,147
Padre Island National Seashore		133,918
TOTAL:		887,286

Agencies: 2 NPS 842,139 + 1 BSFW 45,147

TOTAL—TEXAS		**887,286**

UTAH

Arches N.P.		82,953
Bear River Migratory Bird Refuge		—
Bryce Canyon N.P.		36,010
Capitol Reef N.P.		254,242
Cedar Breaks N.M.		6,155
Dinosaur N.M. (includes acreage in Colorado)		206,663
High Uintas P.A.		237,177
Zion N.P.		147,035
TOTAL:		970,235

Agencies: 1 FS 237,177 + 6 NPS 733,058

TOTAL—UTAH		**970,235**

Name of Area	Placed in NWPS (date) (acres)	Under Review by Agency or Congress (approx. acres)
VIRGINIA		
Cumberland Gap National Historical Park (see also Kentucky and Tennessee)		7,478
Shenandoah N.P.		193,537
TOTAL:		201,015
Agencies: 2 NPS 201,015		
TOTAL—VIRGINIA		**201,015**

Name of Area	Placed in NWPS (date) (acres)	Under Review by Agency or Congress (approx. acres)
WASHINGTON[1]		
Glacier Peak Wilderness (1964)	464,741	
Goat Rocks Wilderness (1964)	82,680	
Jones Island N.W.R.		188
Matia Island N.W.R.		145
Mount Adams Wilderness (1964)	42,411	
Mount Rainier N.P.		241,992
North Cascades N.P.		505,000
Olympic N.P.		896,599
Pasayten Wilderness (1968)	518,000	
San Juan N.W.R.		53
Smith Island N.W.R.		65
Washington Islands Wilderness (1970)		
Copalis N.W.R.	5	

[1] **Cougar Lakes Wilderness** (proposed) North Unit 60,000 acres and South Unit 160,000 acres in Snoqualmie and Gifford Pinchot National Forests, introduced in Congress without agency proposal.

Name of Area	Placed in NWPS (date) (acres)	Under Review by Agency or Congress (approx. acres)
Flattery Rocks N.W.R.	125	
Quillayute Needles N.W.R.	49	
TOTAL:	1,108,011	1,644,042

Agencies: 4 FS 1,107,832 + 3 NPS 1,643,591 + 7 BSFW 630

TOTAL—WASHINGTON   **2,752,053**

WEST VIRGINIA[1,2,3]

[1]**Cranberry Wilderness** (proposed) 36,300 acres

[2]**Otter Creek Wilderness** (proposed) 18,000 acres

[3]**Dolly Sods Wilderness** (proposed) 10,215 acres

All in Monongahela National Forest, introduced in Congress without agency proposals.

WISCONSIN

	Placed in NWPS	Under Review
Wisconsin Island Wilderness (1970)		
(Gravel Island N.W.R.)	27	
(Green Bay N.W.R.)	2	
Upper Mississippi N.W.R. (islands) (see also Illinois, Iowa, Minnesota)		88,000
TOTAL:	29	88,000

Agencies: 3 BSFW 88,029

TOTAL—WISCONSIN   **88,029**

Name of Area	Placed in NWPS (date) (acres)	Under Review by Agency or Congress (approx. acres)

WYOMING[1,2]

Name of Area	Placed in NWPS (date) (acres)	Under Review by Agency or Congress (approx. acres)
Bridger Wilderness (1964)	383,300	
Cloud Peak P.A.		137,000
Glacier P.A.		177,000
Grand Teton N.P.		310,443
North Absaroka Wilderness (1964)	351,104	
Popo Agie P.A.		70,000
South Absaroka Wilderness (1964)	483,678	
Teton Wilderness (1964)	563,500	
Washakie Wilderness (Stratified P.A.)		203,930
Yellowstone N.P. (see also Idaho and Montana)		2,039,217
TOTAL:	1,781,582	2,937,590

Agencies: 8 FS 2,369,512 + 2 NPS 2,349,660

TOTAL—WYOMING   **4,719,172**

[1] **Gros Ventre Wilderness** (proposed) 145,550 acres in Teton N.F., introduced in Congress without agency proposal.

[2] **Laramie Peak Wilderness** (proposed) 25,000 acres in Medicine Bow N.F., introduced in Congress without agency proposal.

Name of Area	Placed in NWPS (date) (acres)	Under Review by Agency or Congress (approx. acres)

Summary

Present and Potential Units of the National Wilderness Preservation System:

			No. of Areas
Acreage in NWPS:			
USFS	10,190,036		62
NPS	93,503		2
BSFW	92,609		17
		10,376,148	81
Acreage Under Review by Agency or Congress:			
USFS	4,397,145		28
NPS	27,219,288		63
BSFW	25,233,003		76
		56,849,436	
		67,225,584	248*

*Not including 16 "De facto" areas proposed for wilderness status (approx. 1,620,065 acres).

APPENDIX C

MICHIGAN'S STATE WILDERNESS BILL

A bill to create and regulate wilderness areas, wild areas and natural areas; to prescribe the functions of certain state officers; to require the promulgation of rules; and to prescribe penalties.

THE PEOPLE OF THE STATE OF MICHIGAN ENACT:

Sec. 1. This act shall be known and may be cited as the "wilderness and natural areas act of 1971".

Sec. 2. As used in this act:

(a) "Board" means the wilderness and natural areas advisory board created pursuant to section 3.

(b) "Commission" means the commission of natural resources.

(c) "Department" means the department of natural resources.

(d) "Wilderness area" means a tract of undeveloped state land under control of the department and dedicated and regulated by the commission pursuant to this act which:

(i) Is 3,000 or more acres in size or is an island of any size.

(ii) Generally appears to have been affected primarily by the forces of nature with the imprint of man's work substantially unnoticeable.

(iii) May have outstanding opportunities for solitude or an unconfined type of recreation.

(iv) Contains ecological, geological or other features of scientific, scenic or historical value.

(e) "Wild area" means a tract of undeveloped state land under control of the department and dedicated and regulated by the commission pursuant to this act which:

(i) Is less than 3,000 acres in size.

(ii) Has outstanding opportunities for personal exploration, challenge or contact with natural features of the landscape.

(iii) Possesses 1 or more of the characteristics of a wilderness area.

(f) "Natural area" means a tract of state land under control of the department and dedicated and regulated by the commission pursuant to this act which:

(i) Has retained or reestablished its natural character, or has unusual flora and fauna or biotic, geologic, scenic or other similar features of educational or scientific value, but it need not be undisturbed.

(ii) Has been identified and verified through research and study by qualified observers.

(iii) May be coextensive with or part of a wilderness area or wild area.

Sec. 3. (1) The wilderness and natural areas advisory board is created within the department of natural resources. The board shall consist of 7 citizens of the state who shall be appointed by the governor with the advice and consent of the senate. Each member shall possess experience in the evaluation and preservation of wilderness or natural areas. The board shall elect 1 of its members as chairman. Members shall serve for terms of 3 years each except that of the members first appointed, 2 shall be appointed for terms of 1 year, 2 for terms of 2 years and 3 for terms of 3 years. Members shall serve without compensation.

(2) The board shall make recommendations for the dedication and administration of wilderness areas, wild areas and natural areas in accordance with this act. The board shall enlist the voluntary cooperation and support of interested citizens and conservation groups.

Sec. 4. (1) Within 6 months after the effective date of this act, and each year thereafter, the department shall review all state land under its control and shall identify those tracts which in its judgment best exhibit the characteristics of a wilderness area, wild area or natural area. The department shall propose to the commission land which in its judgment is most suitable for dedication by the commission as wilderness areas, wild areas or natural areas. The department shall administer the proposed land so as to protect its natural values.

(2) The board or a citizen may propose to the commission land which in its judgment exhibits the characteristics of a wilderness area, wild area or natural area and is suitable for dedication by the commission as such or may propose the alteration or withdrawal of previously dedicated areas. The proposals of the board shall be filed with both houses of the legislature.

(3) Within 90 days after land is proposed in accordance with subsections (1) or (2) the commission shall promulgate a rule making the dedication or issue a written statement of its principal reasons for denying the proposal. The commission shall dedicate a wilderness area, wild area or natural area, or alter or withdraw the dedication by promulgating a rule in accordance with and subject to Act No. 306 of the Public Acts of 1969, as amended, being

sections 24.201 to 24.315 of the Compiled Laws of 1948. All persons who have notified the commission in writing during a calendar year of their interest in dedication of areas under this act shall be furnished by the commission with a notice of all areas pending dedication during that calendar year.

Sec. 5. The commission shall attempt to provide insofar as possible, wild areas and natural areas in relative proximity to urban centers.

Sec. 6. The following are prohibited in a wilderness area, wild area or natural area or in land proposed by the department or the board during the 90 days a dedication is pending pursuant to section 4:

(a) Removing, cutting, picking or otherwise altering vegetation except as necessary for appropriate public access, the preservation or restoration of a plant or wildlife species, or the documentation of scientific values and with written consent of the department.

(b) Condemnation for any purpose.

(c) Granting an easement for any purpose.

(d) Exploration for or extraction of minerals.

(e) A commercial enterprise, utility or permanent road.

(f) A temporary road, landing of aircraft, use of motor vehicles, motorboats, or other form of mechanical transport, or any structure or installation, except as necessary to meet minimum emergency requirements for administration as a wilderness area, wild area or natural area by the department.

(g) Trapping and hunting when recommended by the department.

Sec. 7. A person who lands an aircraft or operates a motor vehicle, motorboat or other form of mechanical transport in a wilderness area, wild area or natural area without the express written consent of the department is guilty of a misdemeanor.

Sec. 8. (1) Land in a wilderness area, wild area or natural area shall be maintained or restored so as to preserve its natural values in a manner compatible with this act.

(2) Waters of this state or marshlands which are an integral part of a wilderness area, wild area or natural area shall be included within and administered as a part of the area.

Sec. 9. The department shall post signs in conspicuous locations along the borders of a wilderness area, wild area or natural area. The signs shall give notice of the area's dedication and shall state those activities which are prohibited pursuant to section 6 and those activities which are punishable as a misdemeanor pursuant to section 7.

Sec. 10. The department may acquire land through purchase, gift or bequest for inclusion in a wilderness area, wild area or natural area.

Sec. 11. (1) Nothing in this act shall be construed to affect or diminish any right acquired or vested before the effective date of this act.

(2) Nothing in this act shall alter the status of lands dedicated by the commission before the effective date of this act until dedicated pursuant to section 4.

About the Sierra Club

The Sierra Club, founded in 1892 by John Muir, has consistently devoted itself to the study and protection of America's scenic resources and wild places. Sierra Club publications are part of the nonprofit effort the club carries on as a public trust. There are chapters in all parts of the United States. Participation is invited in the club's program to enjoy and preserve wilderness, wildlife, and a quality environment for all men, for all time.

Part of the club program aims to service the growing student environmental movement on the nation's campuses. Information on organizational techniques, ecotactics and community action is available from The Campus Program, Sierra Club, Mills Tower, San Francisco, California 94104.

The Sierra Club
Mills Tower
San Francisco, California 94104

Please enroll me as a member of the Sierra Club:

Name _____

Address _____

City, state, zip _____

Dues: $5 admission, plus $15 (regular membership), $7.50 (spouse) or $8 (full-time students, age 15 through 23).

I enclose _____

(We must have this information if applicant is student)

Birthdate _____

School and location _____